HOW TO TRUSS A

Chicken

Text by Michael Powell
Layout by Bag of Badgers Ltd

ISBN 9781552679074.

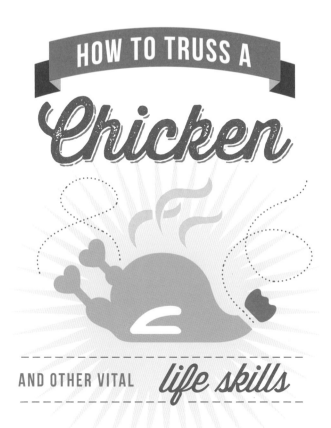

HOW TO TRUSS A

Chicken

AND OTHER VITAL *life skills*

SJG
Gift Publishing

CONTENTS

A cornucopia of life skills to learn!

Introduction

THERE'S A RIGHT AND A WRONG WAY TO DO
EVERYTHING, BUT THERE'S ALWAYS A BETTER
WAY. JUST BECAUSE YOU'VE BEEN PACKING
SUITCASES AND CARVING TURKEYS FOR YEARS,
DOESN'T MEAN THAT YOU'RE ANY BETTER THAN
MEDIOCRE. THE SAME GOES FOR WRAPPING A
GIFT, MOWING THE LAWN OR UNBLOCKING A SINK.
MOST OF US ARE ALARMINGLY INEPT WHEN IT
COMES TO THE SIMPLEST TASKS. WE WOULD ALL
BENEFIT FROM A CRASH COURSE IN HOUSEHOLD
MAINTENANCE AND MANAGEMENT.

Nothing is more important than getting back to basics!
Nothing! That's why you'll love this book. It's an indispensable
collection of practical, straightforward advice – everything you
need to start facing the challenges of domestic life. It even
shows you how to make one great cocktail, because when
you've spent the day doing chores, you deserve to put your
feet up and treat yourself.

It is a pocket compendium of more than seventy domestic skills to boost your home basics, from making bread and preserving flowers to hanging shelves and shovelling snow. Keep it handy so that you can refer to it whenever you need to shuck an oyster, hold a baby, reduce snoring, cold smoke cheese or get rid of woodworm. It's reassuring to discover that many seemingly complicated tasks are quite simple when broken down into their basic essential steps.

Some of the skills in this book require a bit of practice, but in the words of eighties pop band The Korgis, 'everybody's got to learn sometime' and everybody's got to start somewhere too. Even an expert has to begin with the nuts and bolts. Despite this, the hope is that you could actually study topics like 'eat a lobster' or 'make jam' and feel informed and proficient enough to give them a go, although please note that where indicated, some of the medical topics are not a substitute for proper first aid training.

Reading this book won't make you a genius homemaker overnight but it will certainly put you ahead of the game, point you in the right direction and show that some of the skills you considered beyond your reach are extremely accessible.

TRUSS A chicken

TRUSSING YOUR CHICKEN INVOLVES TYING IT UP TO PRESS THE LEGS INTO THE BODY SO THAT THE CHICKEN IS ONE SOLID UNIT. THIS ENSURES THAT THE MEAT COOKS EVENLY AND THAT THE MORE DELICATE WHITE MEAT OF THE BREAST REMAINS MOIST WHILE THE LEGS ARE COOKING. IT ALSO CLOSES THE ENTRANCE TO THE BREAST CAVITY, REDUCING THE AMOUNT OF HOT AIR CIRCULATING INSIDE THE BIRD IN THE OVEN, WHICH ALLOWS THE BREAST TO RETAIN MORE MOISTURE.

1. Place the chicken on a clean kitchen surface or chopping board, breast up, with the legs and body cavity facing away from you.

2. Tuck in the wing tips: holding the tips, open the wings a little and then bring the tips over and under so that they twist over the rest of the wing, then close the wings and press them into the body.

3. Take a long piece of butcher's twine (about 75 cm/30 in long). Place the centre of the string under the bottom, then take an end in each hand and pull vertically, cross the string where the ankles meet, switch hands and pull tight to make a V shape.

4. Keeping the tension in the V, loop the right string under the right ankle followed by the left string underneath the left ankle and then pull your hands horizontally away from each other so the ankles press tightly against the bottom and the thighs sit snugly against the breast.

5. Now bring the string along the side of each thigh, underneath each wing, making sure you keep the string tight and then tie a knot underneath the neck.

6. The chicken should now be a single solid unit, with wings tucked in and thighs firmly tucked against the body.

7. Cut off any excess string and the chicken is ready for roasting.

Jump start a vehicle

JUMP STARTING A VEHICLE IS EASY BUT YOU
SHOULD ONLY DO IT IF YOUR BATTERY IS DEAD
AND YOU MUST PERFORM CERTAIN STEPS IN
THE CORRECT ORDER OR YOU RISK GETTING AN
ELECTRIC SHOCK OR DAMAGING BOTH CARS.

To check whether your battery is dead, switch on the
headlights. If they are dim or don't light at all, the battery
is dead. If the lights are bright, your battery is fine and the
problem may be with your ignition.

1. Locate the battery (in some cars the battery is in the boot)
   and check that the terminals are in good order. Remove
   corrosion or rust with a wire brush.

2. Don't jump start if the battery is cracked or leaking, or has
   been unused for several days, since there could be a build-
   up of flammable hydrogen. Don't smoke and keep away
   from naked flames.

3. Batteries contain sulphuric acid, so wear protective gloves
   and goggles. If you get battery acid on your skin, wash
   immediately with lots of cold water.

4. Park the car with a good battery close to yours but not
   touching. Make sure the batteries are the same voltage.

5. Apply the handbrakes and turn off both ignitions and all peripheral electrical features such as air-conditioning, radio and lights.

6. Connect the jump leads in this order and do not let red and black leads touch:

    a. clamp one end of the red jump lead to the positive terminal (POS or +) on the dead battery

    b. clamp the other end of the red jump lead to the positive terminal (POS or +) on the good battery

    c. clamp one end of the black jump lead to the negative terminal (NEG or -) on the good battery

    d. clamp the other end of the black jump lead to the engine block of the dead car, well away from the battery. This earths the circuit.

7. Make sure the jump leads are not touching any moving parts.

8. Start the engine of the good car and let it idle for one minute.

9. Start the engine of the dead car. If it fails, wait ten seconds and try again. If it doesn't start after four or five attempts, stop or you could damage the starter motor.

10. If the engine starts, leave both cars running and remove the jump cables in reverse order (d), (c), (b), (a).

11. Drive for at least 30 minutes to charge the battery or use a battery charger when you get home. If the battery won't charge, you may need a new battery or alternator.

IRON A SHIRT AND PRESS TROUSERS

IRONING A SHIRT AND TROUSERS
SHOULDN'T TAKE MORE THAN SIX MINUTES
AND WON'T BE IRKSOME IF YOU USE A CLEAN
STEAM IRON WITH A WIDE IRONING BOARD
(THE WIDER THE BETTER).

SHIRT

1. Check the care label for the correct ironing temperature.

2. It is very difficult to remove the creases from a bone dry garment, so iron the shirt while it is a little damp or use a mist sprayer to damp it down.

3. Press with the heel of the iron rather than the front, otherwise you will end up with little ripples on the material that will be hard to remove. Keep steaming regularly to relax the fibres.

4. Iron the back of the collar first, then the front, ironing in from the edges. Then fold the collar down, give a quick steam on the centre back of the collar and then do up the top button (this helps the shirt to stay on the board).

5. Open the cuffs and iron them inside and then outside, working in from the edges. Don't make a crease; the cuffs should form a smooth hollow tube.

6. Smooth the sleeves flat to avoid creases and iron once with the seams parallel. Pull on the cuffs to keep the sleeve material taut and flat as you iron.

7. Lay the shirt face down on the board and iron from the shoulders (the 'yoke') to the shirt tail.

8. Iron the right front panel. Press the tip of the iron in between the buttons while you pull the material tight. Then iron the back and roll the shirt round to iron the left front panel.

9. Leave the shirt to cool down on a hanger for ten minutes before wearing.

TROUSERS

1. The key to creating a good crease is to press trousers, not iron them. Always press down rather than moving the iron from side to side, otherwise you will give the material an unwanted shine.

2. Turn the trousers inside out and iron the pockets, flies and hems. Then turn right side out again.

3. Place the waistband over the edge of the board and press the top of the trousers, then lay the trousers out flat along the board, with the fly facing away from you.

4. Fold away the top (right) leg so that you can work on the bottom (left) leg. Work on the front crease first (farthest

away from you). Line up the seams and then press a crease once at the bottom of the leg. Then, keeping the leg flat, press in a front crease along the whole leg from hem to top of the leg, stopping about 16 cm/6¼ in from the waistband on flat-fronted trousers; if the trousers are pleated run the crease into the pleat.

5. Go back to the hem and press the back crease working from hem to top of the leg, then gently press over the centre of the trouser (on the seam).

6. Turn the trousers over, fold over the top leg and repeat the process with the other leg (the front crease will now be facing you).

7. For a really sharp crease, use an old tailoring trick of banging and pressing the crease with an unvarnished wooden block (e.g. the smooth back of a scrubbing brush) immediately after you have pressed the crease, to drive the steam out.

8. Hang the trousers up immediately and allow them to cool and dry for half an hour before wearing.

Stem a haemorrhage

Bleeding cuts or wounds require decisive action as the loss of just two pints of blood can cause a person to go into shock and suffer a life-threatening drop in blood pressure.

1. Call emergency services for an abdominal or chest wound or if the bleeding is severe, you suspect internal bleeding, blood is spurting out or cannot be stopped after ten minutes of firm and steady pressure.

2. Apply direct pressure on the wound with a clean cloth or tissue until bleeding stops. If blood soaks through, don't change the cloth; maintain pressure and add another cloth on top.

3. If the arm or leg is bleeding, raise the limb above the heart to slow the bleeding.

4. Don't use a tourniquet unless the bleeding is severe.

5. When the bleeding has stopped, clean the wound with soap and warm water, apply antiseptic cream and cover with a sterile bandage.

6. Seek medical help if the wound is deep and/or jagged (it may need stitches), has ingrained dirt or debris or if it becomes infected (red, tender, oozes discharge or the injured person has a temperature) or feels numb.

Treat stings and bruises

MOST STINGS AND BRUISES CAN BE TREATED AT HOME BUT IF YOU EXPERIENCE SEVERE SYMPTOMS, SEEK IMMEDIATE MEDICAL ATTENTION. THE QUICKER YOU ACT THE MORE CHANCE YOU HAVE OF REDUCING THE EFFECTS.

STINGS

1. Remove the stinger and venomous sac quickly and carefully by scraping it with a hard edge, such as a knife, fingernail or bank card. Don't squeeze the stinger out as this will cause more tissue damage and force more venom into the wound.

2. Wash the affected area with soap and warm water; this reduces the risk of infection and removes venom at the surface of the skin.

3. Apply a cold compress to reduce the swelling (don't place ice directly on the wound).

4. Don't scratch; this increases the risk of infection. Some sources advise lightly tapping the site to break up the venom and to reduce the itching.

5. If you develop a blister, do not pop it as this exposes the broken skin to infection. Use an adhesive bandage to protect the area.

6. Apply sting cream or spray that contains local anaesthetic, antihistamine or mild hydrocortisone to reduce itching and swelling; if none are available you can make your own by mixing a little baking soda with water.

7. You may take painkillers, such as paracetamol or ibuprofen and/or an antihistamine tablet to reduce swelling

BRUISES

A bruise is caused by damage to tiny blood vessels underneath your skin. Most bruises stop being painful after a few days and disappear within a few weeks, but early intervention can ease your symptoms.

1. Apply a cold compress (a bag of frozen peas or a tea towel filled with crushed ice) for fifteen minutes. This constricts the blood vessels and reduces the blood flow to the damaged area. Don't waste a prime piece of steak; the only benefit of holding a steak against a black eye is the coldness of the meat.

2. Rest the affected area and keep it raised.

3. Apply anti-bruising creams such as a vitamin K or arnica cream. Witch hazel is an effective natural remedy that has been used on cuts and bruises for centuries.

4. The day after a bruise develops, apply a heat pack or a flannel soaked in warm water to the area several times a day. This helps to dissolve and dissipate the blood that has gathered underneath the skin.

AVOID AND TREAT A HANGOVER

THE BEST WAY TO AVOID A HANGOVER IS TO DRINK IN MODERATION, BUT IF YOU INSIST ON OVER-INDULGING, THESE COUNTERMEASURES WILL REDUCE THE DAMAGE TO BRAIN AND BODY.

BEFORE YOU HEAD OUT FOR THE NIGHT

1. Never drink on an empty stomach. Eat some fatty, carbohydrate-rich food such as pizza or pasta to reduce the speed at which the alcohol is broken down in your stomach, so it will enter your bloodstream more slowly. If you want a healthier alternative, line your stomach with some oily fish such as salmon and swig a tablespoon of olive oil.

2. Take a multivitamin. Alcohol destroys B vitamins and your body uses a lot of nutrients to help break down the alcohol.

WHILE YOU'RE OUT

1. Alcoholic drinks contain lots of other chemicals apart from alcohol; these 'convenors' improve taste and colour, but mixing drinks also mixes convenors, so stick to one kind of drink all night. Avoid cocktails, which are particularly lethal.

2. Light-coloured drinks usually contain fewer convenors, so white wine or vodka should give you an easier time.

3. Go easy on anything with bubbles, especially champagne, as this speeds up the entry of alcohol into the bloodstream.

4. An enzyme in your liver breaks down the alcohol to acetaldehyde then acetic acid and finally to carbon dioxide and water. Your body can only break down one unit of alcohol per hour, so if you exceed this the excess acetaldehyde reaches the bloodstream causing cell and even DNA damage and helps to cause a hangover.

5. Alternate your drinks by having one soft drink (preferably a glass of water) for every alcoholic one. This also helps you to stay hydrated (dehydration is a major factor in a hangover).

BEFORE YOU GO TO BED

1. Drink two pints of water and eat a little food that will release energy slowly throughout the night such as protein, fatty foods, citrus and vegetables.

2. Take another multivitamin and avoid painkillers.

IN THE MORNING

1. Drink lots of water and avoid caffeinated drinks such as coffee or colas, which will dehydrate you.

2. Alcohol affects your body's ability to regulate its temperature, so stay cool and don't overexert yourself.

REDUCE SNORING

SNORING IS CAUSED BY THE VIBRATION OF THE SOFT PALATE AND OTHER TISSUE IN THE MOUTH, NOSE AND THROAT. INDIVIDUALS SNORE FOR DIFFERENT REASONS BUT TWO OF THE MOST COMMON FACTORS ARE BEING OVERWEIGHT AND NOT TAKING ENOUGH EXERCISE.

Snoring can get worse with age as muscle tone decreases and airways become narrower. Men have naturally narrower airways than women and they tend to put on weight around their necks and waist, so men are more prone to snoring than women. Here are some of the ways you can help yourself.

1. Lose weight. Even carrying an extra ten kilos can trigger snoring. Losing weight will reduce the size of the soft palate and reduce fat around the neck.

2. Exercise regularly. Toning up your arms, legs and core body strength and improving your cardiovascular fitness has a knock-on effect to other parts of your body and can help to tone up the weak muscles in your throat.

3. A study carried out by the Royal Devon and Exeter Hospital has shown that snoring can be reduced by singing. Subjects spent three months working with choir director, singer and composer Alise Ojay, who has developed the 'Singing for Snorers' programme. His set of daily vocal exercises (such as singing the sounds 'ung' and 'gar') has been shown to firm up the pharyngeal muscles and reduce snoring.

4. Learn to play the didgeridoo. Studies show that playing this native Australian wind instrument strengthens the soft palate and throat, reducing snoring.

5. Avoid drinking alcohol or taking sleeping pills or sedatives before going to sleep. This increases muscle relaxation and constricts the nasal passages.

6. Change your sleeping position. Lie on your side and avoid sleeping on your back. This reduces the likelihood of the tongue and soft tissues dropping to obstruct your airway.

7. Use an extra pillow to elevate your head to ease breathing and allow your tongue and jaw to move forward.

8. Smoking has been found to disrupt sleep and contribute to snoring by irritating the lining of the nasal cavity.

9. Use a humidifier to keep bedroom air moist; dry air can irritate the nose and throat.

10. Close your mouth and try to breathe through your nose. Use a chin strap to keep your mouth closed and a nasal strip to increase the air flow through your nose.

Decorate a Christmas tree

CLASSY-LOOKING CHRISTMAS DECORATIONS ARE EXPENSIVE AND IT CAN TAKE YEARS TO AMASS A DECENT COLLECTION, UNLESS YOU WANT TO BLOW YOUR ENTIRE YULETIDE BUDGET AT ONCE. HOWEVER, REGARDLESS OF HOW MUCH CASH YOU CAN SPLASH ON YOUR FESTIVE DECKING, FOLLOWING THESE SIMPLE RULES WILL GIVE YOU THE BEST RESULTS.

1. Choosing the right tree is the crucial first step. Make sure you see the tree freestanding and unwrapped, so that you can check it is vertical and symmetrical.

2. When you get the tree home, saw 5 cm/2 in off the bottom and erect it away from a radiator, using a stand that can hold water. Keeping the water level topped up will greatly reduce needle loss. Prune the branches to correct any asymmetry.

3. Add the lights first. Check they are working and then arrange them from the base upwards, placing lights on every major

branch on the inside and middle of the branches rather than the tips, to give density and depth and to hide the wires. Stand back regularly and squint to spot and correct any bare patches.

4. Use at least 200 LED lights for every vertical metre of tree. Static white or off-white lights usually look better than a flashing multicoloured melee. Smaller pinpoint (LED) lights work better than huge candles or globes, because they should provide accent rather than dominate.

5. Next add any tinsel, richly textured ribbon, garlands and deco mesh. Hang these items loosely so they drape and curve. Use less at the top of the tree otherwise it will look top heavy.

6. Finally add your ornaments. Choose one or two complimentary colours and decide whether your want a warm theme (orange, red, gold) or cold (blue, white, silver).

7. Place your large baubles first, about ten every half metre of tree, then fill in between with the smaller ones. Place some ornaments inside the tree to give depth.

8. Don't hang baubles below the bottom of the tree. End them at the bottom of the foliage for a robust solid effect, rather than a piecemeal straggly silhouette.

9. You can also add natural features such as pine cones, feathers, twigs, dried fruit and spices which can add fragrance as well as visual variety.

10. Use a feature decoration at the top – star, angel, etc.

Wrap a gift

FIRST IMPRESSIONS COUNT, SO THE CARE WITH WHICH YOU WRAP A GIFT CAN HAVE GREATER IMPACT THAN THE GIFT ITSELF. EVEN THOUGH YOU HAVE TAKEN THE TIME TO GO ONLINE AND CLICK 'BUY' AND HAVE PARTED WITH YOUR HARD-EARNED CASH, WRAPPING A GIFT IS YOUR CHANCE TO ADD THE PERSONAL FINISHING TOUCH.

1. Thick paper looks better than thinner paper. You may try to compensate for thin, cheap paper by double wrapping, but your gift still won't look professional without thick, classy wrapping with crisp, well-defined seams. So always spend a little bit extra on the wrapping.

2. When wrapping an irregular-shaped object, place it in a box. Boxes are easier to wrap and they conform to the idealized shape of a gift.

3. Place the box on the paper and cut it to size first. Allow for about 10 cm/4 in overlap on top, and the sides should be about three-quarters of the height of the box. If you leave too much paper on the edges they will be bulky and unsightly.

4. Wrap around the long edge first. Place the object in the centre of the paper, bring one long end over to the top of the box and tape this end to the box, so that the paper doesn't slip around; this allows you to get a nice tight fit. Press along the edges to define the seams.

5. Now fold the ends. Press the top end down flat against the first side and crease two triangles to form side flaps. Fold these flaps in, creasing along the bottom seam so that the paper stays tight against the contours of the box to leave you with a bottom triangular flap. Crease this and bring the flap up to meet the top flap and tape. Repeat with the other open end.

6. Wrap a ribbon lengthwise all around the box, keeping it tight against the box. Press your thumb on top of the ribbon in the middle of the box, take the ribbon once around the short side and then tuck the ribbon diagonally underneath the meeting point and pull tight. To make the bow, form a loop in each hand and bring one loop over the other to form a knot.

7. Cut the two ribbon edges at 45 degrees and then make them curl by running them between your thumb and the edge of a pair of scissors.

HOLD A BABY

HOLDING A BABY CAN BE OVERWHELMING IF YOU'VE NEVER DONE IT BEFORE, NOT LEAST BECAUSE THEY SEEM SO FRAGILE.

Your biggest concern will undoubtedly be not hurting the baby, but actually they are much more sturdy than they appear. You can't go far wrong with a young baby so long as you support the head, neck and spine. There are lots of ways of cuddling a baby, apart from at arm's length.

CRADLE HOLD

This is a very easy and natural position. Close your arm against your body, rest the baby's head and neck in the crook of your elbow, support the back with your forearm and place your hand underneath the bottom to support some more weight and to prevent the baby from wriggling free.

When taking a baby from someone else's cradle hold, take the baby with both hands, one supporting the head and neck and the other supporting the bottom and lower back. Take the baby close to your body and then gently slide your arm so that the baby's head comes to rest in the crook of your elbow.

Even though the baby may weigh less than five kilos, your arm can easily become tired, so you might want to change position and hold the baby with your other arm. To switch position, support the head with your free hand, while keeping your other arm and hand on the back and bottom, then move your arms away from your body and rotate the baby until it is resting on your other arm.

SNUGGLE HOLD

From cradle hold, rotate the baby so that it is facing into your chest. Hold the baby with one hand under the bottom and the other behind the head to support the neck and head. Then move the baby up to the lower part of your shoulder. Babies love this position because they can hear your breathing and heart beat. Make sure the baby's head is turned to one side so it can breathe easily.

LAP HOLD

Sit down with your knees closed and your feet flat on the floor. Place the baby on its back with the head supported in your hands and its back supported by your thighs.

BELLY HOLD

The baby lies face down on your forearm with its head by your elbow and with your hand between its legs so that it is fully supported. This is a good position for relieving wind.

SET THE TABLE

WHETHER YOU WANT TO HAVE A DINNER GATHERING FOR DIGNITARIES OR KICK BACK WITH A FEW CLOSE FRIENDS, FOLLOW THESE SIMPLE TABLE-SETTING RULES FOR ELEGANT DINING.

1. Cover the table with a white linen tablecloth so the centre crease runs in a straight line down the middle of the table. The ends of the tablecloth should overhang the table by about 45 cm/18 in (for a buffet it should reach the floor).

2. Fold the napkins and place them in the centre of each place setting (alternatively, place them to the left of the forks). With a triangular napkin, the longest straight edge faces the plate and the point faces left.

3. Position the cutlery about 2.5 cm/1 in from the edge of the table with the first course cutlery on the outside and the

final course cutlery on the inside. Diners begin at the outside and work in.

4. Knives go on the right of the plate, with the cutting edge facing the plate; if there is a fish course, the fish knife goes to the right of this. Forks go on the left of the plate with the tines facing upwards. The salad fork goes on the outside, followed by the main course fork. A dessert fork can either be placed to the right of the main course fork or horizontally above the plate.

5. The soup spoon is placed to the right of the knives, or it may arrive with the soup course; the dessert spoon sits horizontally above the plate, pointing to the left.

6. The bread and butter plate sits at a northwest position relative to the dinner plate, with a butter knife resting horizontally across the top of it, with the blade pointing to the left and the cutting edge facing the diner.

7. Stemware is set above and to the right of the dinner plate, again in order of use: water glass about 5 cm/2 in above the main course knife; the white wine glass is to its right and the red wine glass top centre. The champagne glass is at the far right.

8. Specialist cutlery such as escargot holders, lobster pliers and shell fish picks can be brought to the table with the appropriate course.

Stop a nosebleed

NOSEBLEEDS ARE FAIRLY COMMON, PARTICULARLY DURING CHILDHOOD. MOST ARE MINOR AND CAN BE TREATED AT HOME.

You should only seek medical attention if you have heavy or frequent nosebleeds, are taking blood thinning medication or if the bleeding lasts longer than 30 minutes.

WHAT CAUSES A NOSEBLEED?

The inside of your nose has lots of tiny blood vessels. If conditions are very arid, the inside of the nose can dry out and the mucous membrane can become encrusted, inflamed or cracked, causing bleeding. The blood vessels can also be damaged by trauma such as an impact injury or even nose picking.

Nosebleeds usually stop of their own accord, but here's how to make yourself more comfortable and speed up the healing process.

1. Stay calm and still. Don't do anything to raise your blood pressure or make your heart beat faster as this will only pump blood out of your nose more quickly.

2. Sit down and tilt your head forward to stop blood running down your throat (don't tilt your head backwards). Breathe through your mouth.

3. Pinch your nose between thumb and forefinger and apply pressure to the nasal septum (the piece of cartilage that runs down the middle of the inside of the nose and separates the nostrils).

4. Press an ice pack or a bag of frozen vegetables against your nose.

5. Don't stuff tissue or cotton balls up your nose to stem the blood flow as this will only increase the pressure in your nose and might give you a headache.

6. Place a small piece of wet tissue in between your top teeth and lip then press your lip over the tissue.

AFTER THE NOSEBLEED HAS STOPPED

1. If the nosebleed was caused by dry air, increase the humidity in the room by boiling a kettle or taking a shower, or spray a fine mist in front of your face and take a few breaths through your nose to moisten the inside.

2. Don't pick or blow your nose. Wait a few hours before attempting to remove any blood clots.

3. For at least 24 hours, avoid any strenuous activity that will raise your blood pressure and increase the risk of bleeding.

4. When lying down, use an extra pillow so your head stays higher than your heart to decrease nasal pressure.

FIX A DRIPPING TAP

THERE ARE SEVERAL REASONS WHY A TAP MAY BE LEAKING, BUT THE MOST COMMON CAUSES ARE OLD GASKETS, 'O'-RINGS (LEAKING HANDLE) OR CORRODED SEAT VALVES AND WASHERS.

TURN OFF THE WATER

Turn off the water supply and open the tap to run off water in the pipes. The mains stopcock is usually underneath the kitchen sink, or outside. The hot water stopcock will be near the boiler or hot water tank. Before turning off the hot water, switch off the heating system, otherwise when you run off the water you'll be heating empty pipes which will burn out the heater.

If the water is still trickling slightly out of the tap, you haven't turned the stopcock tightly enough. Only strip down the tap when the water flow has stopped completely. Also, put the plug in the sink or bathtub so you don't lose any small screws, nuts or bolts down the drain.

STRIP DOWN THE TAP

On some taps the handle is attached with a screw. Unscrew and remove the handle to reveal the tap stem and bonnet beneath. You may have to prise a cap off the handle with a screwdriver to get at the screw.

Use an adjustable wrench to unbolt the bonnet, and then remove the valve system by turning it into the 'off' position while lifting gently upwards. Hold the tap with your other hand to prevent it from twisting and damaging the pipe work beneath.

REPLACE THE COMPONENTS

The washer and 'O'-ring are held in place by a bolt at the bottom of the valve assembly. Undo the bolt and replace them. If the washer is missing, it will be stuck inside the tap, and must be prised out with a screwdriver. Replace with identical-sized washers or 'O'-rings, but don't match old for new, since the old ones will look smaller and thinner due to wear (for example, the hole in the middle will look smaller on a new washer). If in doubt, take the valve system to your hardware store.

Reattach the bolt to secure the washer, and then replace the valve system by lowering and turning gently into the 'on' position. Attach the handle and turn the tap to the 'off' position before turning the water back on at the mains.

SINGLE-LEVER TAPS

Some taps have a single lever which allows you to choose between hot and cold water. These are more difficult to repair and the job often requires specialist tools.

At the bottom of the handle there is a setscrew. Use a hex wrench to undo it and then remove the handle and the ball assembly underneath. Remove and replace the rubber valve seats and steel springs using long-nose pliers. Also make sure that the ball is free from corrosion or limescale.

To reassemble, line up the peg on the side of the hole with the rectangular slot on the ball.

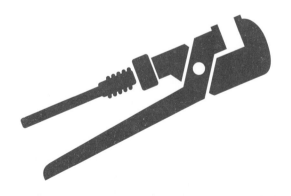

DOUSE A FIRE

It is essential to tackle a fire quickly during the early stages to prevent it getting out of hand.
So remember these three important rules:

1. Personal safety comes first. If the fire has spread to other areas or smoke is at head height, call emergency services and evacuate everyone in the building, including yourself.

2. Do not use water on liquid, electrical or chemical fires.

3. When using a fire extinguisher, aim the nozzle at the base or seat of a fire.

ELECTRICAL FIRE

1. Don't use water. Water conducts electricity, so it will make it worse and increase your risk of electrocution.

2. Turn off the mains electricity.

3. Smother the fire with a safety blanket or use a multipurpose CO_2 or dry powder extinguisher.

LIQUID FIRE (E.G. OIL, PETROL)

1. Don't use water. Water is more dense than many other liquids, so it sinks to the bottom and heats up to become steam, which bursts into the air, scattering the burning liquid.

2. Smother the fire with a wet towel, safety blanket or dry powder extinguisher.

WALLPAPERING CAN BE ONE OF THE MORE DEMANDING DECORATING TASKS, BUT ONCE YOU GET THE HANG OF IT, IT CAN BE QUICKER AND TIDIER THAN PAINTING.

BE PREPARED

1. To work out how many rolls of wallpaper you need, measure the length of each wall and add the figures together. Then multiply that result by the height of the room to get the total area, and add ten per cent. Compare that to the square metre area per roll of wallpaper (it's written on the packet). Don't bother subtracting door and window dimensions, unless a wall is all window.

2. Cut strips 10 cm/4 in longer than you need (or more if you have a large pattern). Fill in holes and cracks and sand the walls until they are smooth and clean. Don't leave any lumps as these will show through the paper.

3. Switch off the electricity and remove switch plates and plugs.

GET HANGING

1. Draw a straight vertical line just over a roll's width away from

one corner using a spirit level. This is where you will hang your first length.

2. Apply the glue to the back of the first strip using a paint roller or large brush, and a wallpapering table. Pay special attention to corners and edges.

3. 'Book' the strip by gathering it up into a concertina and leave for about three minutes to allow the glue to soak in.

4. Un-book the top part of the strip and stick it to the top of the wall, allowing a 5 cm/2 in overlap at the ceiling. Slide the paper gently to line it up with the plumb line. Use a dry brush to press the strip against the wall, then un-book and smooth the bottom half into position.

5. Smooth the whole strip working diagonally from the top down and centre outwards. Prick any remaining air bubbles with a pin and then smooth.

6. Wipe off excess glue with a damp cloth and slowly trim the edges along the ceiling and skirting board with a utility knife (change the blade if the paper begins to tear).

7. Repeat with the second strip, and butt the edge up against the first, but do not overlap. After ten minutes use a seam roller on the seams, but don't force out the glue.

8. To hang around doors and windows, smooth into place first and then make diagonal cuts to allow you to smooth into the corners.

9. Paper over light switches and plug outlets, and then cut a hole slightly smaller than the cover before replacing it.

HANG SHELVES

HANGING SHELVES IS ONE OF THE EASIER DIY TASKS, SO LONG AS YOU MAKE SURE EVERYTHING IS LEVEL AND YOU USE THE CORRECT SIZE OF SCREWS AND RAWL PLUGS TO BEAR THEIR WEIGHT.

BUILT-IN SHELVES

The simplest way to put up shelves is to build them into an alcove (often at the side of a chimney breast). Decide how many you want and space them apart, by drawing lines on the wall using a spirit level. Cut wooden battens to suit the depth of the shelves. You can hide the supports by attaching a lip to the end; if you don't do this, cut the battens so they taper at 45 degrees. Metal side supports look slick and with some systems, the shelf hides the support by sliding into it.

FIXING INDIVIDUAL BRACKETS

Mark two vertical guidelines using a spirit level. Hold one bracket at the right height and mark the wall through the fixing holes. Drill into a solid wall using a masonry bit. If the wall is timber-framed, locate the studs and drill pilot holes for the screws. (Measure out from the corner and tap on the wall with a hammer at locations in multiples of 40 cm/14½ in apart; you will hear hollow sounds between the studs and a solid sound at the stud.) Insert rawl plugs and screw the bracket into place. Use the shelf and spirit level to mark and fix the position of the second bracket.

SHELVING SYSTEMS

The upright supports must be vertical. The best way to ensure that they are is to fix each one lightly to the wall by its top screw, then mark the position of the bottom screw using a spirit level to ensure that it is vertical. To line up the second support, clip one bracket to the upright, then another to the second upright. Lay a shelf across the brackets and use a spirit level to check the shelf is horizontal. Mark the top hole of the second upright and then fix to the wall, marking the bottom screw as before with the help of a spirit level.

GET IN LINE

When you are erecting a bank of shelving, fix all the brackets then line up the shelves using a plumb line before you attach them to the brackets.

SAGGING SHELVES

Shelves sag when the span of the shelf between the two supports is too long, the shelf is too thin, or the load is too heavy. You can fix this by attaching a wall-fixed batten to the back edge, and/or a wooden or metal front lip.

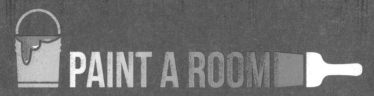

PAINT A ROOM

PAINTING IS THE QUICKEST AND OFTEN THE CHEAPEST WAY OF FRESHENING UP A ROOM OR GIVING IT A COMPLETE MAKEOVER.

CHOOSE YOUR MATERIALS

It is essential to use quality brushes and choose the right paint. Use brushes with a natural bristle or a natural lamb's wool roller for oil-based paint and a synthetic brush or roller for emulsion (natural bristles go limp in water-based paint).

Use matt emulsion for walls and ceilings, vinyl silk for areas of high humidity like bathrooms and kitchens (or for children's bedrooms for ease of wiping clean) and gloss on woodwork. Oil-based paint is stain resistant and is often used in bathrooms and kitchens. Measure the area of walls and ceilings and check coverage on the paint tin so that you don't buy too much. Good quality paint goes onto the wall more smoothly and gives greater coverage and a superior finish.

PREPARE THE SURFACES

Remove all furniture and curtains from the room. Remove dust and cobwebs with a vacuum cleaner and wet cloth, then fill any holes with filler and sand the walls smooth. You should spend as long preparing the surfaces as you do painting. If you strip anything back to the wood or plaster, apply a primer or the paint won't stick. Then give the walls a once-over with a low-phosphate household cleaner or commercial wall-cleaning product to remove stains such as grease or cigarette smoke which will soak through the new paint. Cover the floor with a thick canvas or tarpaulin (avoid using bed sheets as they are too thin and spilled paint will soak through).

APPLY THE PAINT

Ensure there is adequate ventilation, and take regular breaks to avoid inhaling too many paint fumes. Paint the ceiling first, then the walls and finally the woodwork. Paint an 8 cm/3 in strip along the edge of the ceiling where it meets the walls. This is called 'cutting-in'. You can paint the rest of the ceiling using a long-handled roller. Apply a second coat if required only when the first coat is dry.

Next the walls: cut in along the top of the wall then start at the top corner of a wall and work downwards and into the middle. Paint square sections going up and down then across for an even finish. When using a roller avoid stopping in mid-stroke as this will leave a mark.

CLEANING UP

If you spill paint wipe off immediately as it will be harder to remove when it is dry (especially from fabrics).

LAY A CARPET

CARPET LAYING IS OFTEN INCLUDED IN THE PRICE OF THE CARPET, BUT IT'S WELL WORTH DOING YOURSELF AND SPENDING THE MONEY YOU SAVE ON BETTER QUALITY CARPET AND UNDERLAY.

PREPARE THE FLOOR

If you have a wooden floor, nail down any loose floorboards and remove any irregularities such as screws, nails and staples. For concrete or masonry surfaces, make sure they are clean, dry and free from potholes.

LAY THE GRIPPER

Carpet grippers are flat wooden strips with nails sticking out of them and they grip the edges of the carpet. Use gripper shears to cut them to size. Lay the strip about 5 mm/¼ in (a fingertip) away from the edge of the wall and nail into the floor with the little nails facing the wall (there should be an arrow on the gripper to remind you). Don't lay strips across doorways.

Install the underlay with the wavy rubber side down, so that it butts right up to the edge of the carpet gripper (not over it). Butt the edges of the underlay against each other (don't overlap them). Cut the underlay to size in situ by running a utility knife along the floor. Glue the underlay to the floor using superspray adhesive and cover the seams with duct tape.

CUTTING AND POSITIONING

You'll need a carpet fitting kit, consisting of a carpet stretcher, a bolster chisel and a utility knife. Measure the dimensions of the room and cut the carpet to size, allowing about 15 cm/6 in excess for final trimming. Cut so that the pile of the carpet faces the same direction as the pile of any adjacent carpet (usually facing towards the door).

If the carpet is patterned, ensure the pattern is aligned with the main wall or main focal point in the room. Cut pile carpet along the back with a utility knife and cut loop pile carpet from the front.

Once you've positioned the carpet, push any wrinkles to the edges by making a shuffling movement with your feet. Push the carpet right into the corner and make a vertical cut in the corner of the carpet so that it eases into place.

STRETCH THE CARPET

Starting at the corner that is diagonally opposite the doorway, use the carpet stretcher to attach the carpet to the gripper for about one metre in each direction and use a knee kicker to force the carpet forward. Then stretch the carpet in the corner opposite the door for one metre, followed by the longest side (opposite the door), then the corner opposite where you started (on the door wall), and the corner diagonally opposite to where you started, then finally along the door wall and the remaining side. Trim the excess by folding the carpet back on itself and crease it so that it is tight against the skirting board, then cut about 8 mm from the base of the skirting and tuck it underneath the skirting board using the bolster chisel.

When performed correctly, the Heimlich manoeuvre is safe and effective. Here is a step-by-step guide, but this is no substitute for proper first aid training.

PERFORM THE HEIMLICH MANOEUVRE

1. Only use the procedure if you are sure that the person is choking. Ask them if they can speak or cough; if they can, don't use the Heimlich manoeuvre. Do not use it on a child less than a year old.

2. Apply several firm backslaps first. If this fails to remove the airway obstruction, use the Heimlich manoeuvre.

3. Stand the person up, stand behind them and reach your arms around their waist. Find their navel and put your right fist just above that (but below the ribcage).

4. Cup your right fist firmly in your left hand and then pull upwards and inwards in a 'J' shaped motion. This forces air out of the lungs and pops out the blockage by generating an artificial cough.

5. The action should be hard, but not so hard as to cause damage to ribs or internal organs. Take extra care if the person is elderly or a child, as they can be injured more easily.

6. If the person can now speak and cough, the blockage has been removed. If not, repeat the 'J' shaped thrusting movement. If repeated attempts fail to clear the airway, call the emergency services immediately.

MAKE A BED WITH HOSPITAL CORNERS

DESPITE THE POPULARITY OF FITTED SHEETS, FEW SIMPLE PLEASURES ARE MORE SATISFYING THAN MAKING A CRISP AND SMOOTH BED WITH HOSPITAL CORNERS USING A REGULAR SHEET.

1. Lay the bottom sheet over the mattress with the middle crease running down the centre.

2. Tuck under the top of the sheet at the head of the mattress.

3. Starting at the left bottom corner, pull the sheet taut lengthways with your right hand underneath the mattress.

4. With your left hand, lift up the side edge about 30 cm/12 in from the bottom end and bring it onto the bed so the folded edge of the sheet forms a 45-degree angle from that corner on the surface of the bed (resembling the corner of a picture frame).

5. Put your arm on the top corner to keep the edge smooth while you tuck in the remaining little triangle of the sheet that is hanging below the mattress.

6. Now bring the top triangle down, keeping it taut, so that the edge forms a 45-degree angle on the side of the mattress and tuck it underneath the mattress.

7. Repeat on the other three corners making sure that you pull the sheet taut as this tension will also help to keep the tucked in edges in place.

8. Place the top sheet on top of the bed so that the crease runs down the middle. Tuck the bottom two corners as detailed above, or leave it looser, depending on how much foot room you want, then add blankets as required.

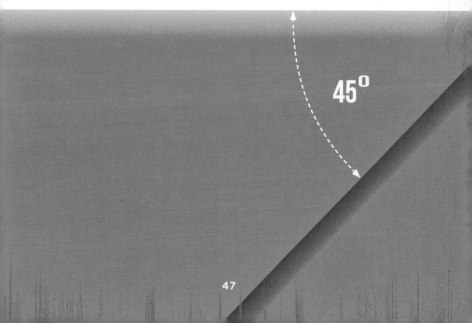

45°

LOBSTER IS NOT ONLY DELICIOUS, IT IS PACKED WITH AMINO ACIDS, A AND B VITAMINS AND MINERALS SUCH AS POTASSIUM, MAGNESIUM, CALCIUM, PHOSPHORUS, IRON AND ZINC. IT IS ALSO LOW IN FAT. HOWEVER, IT IS ADVISABLE TO EAT YOUR LOBSTER OUTDOORS (OR AT LEAST WELL AWAY FROM ANY CARPETS).

1. Break the two large front claws from the body by holding the knuckle and twisting 180 degrees gently while pulling. Break the knuckle and pincer part from the claw, then use a lobster cracker to break the shell of the main part of the claw. Pull the meat out in one or two pieces.

2. Crack the knuckles with the cracker, pull them apart and then pull the meat out using a pick. Alternatively, you can cut them open using poultry shears.

3. The tail is one of the best parts of the lobster. Separate the tail section from the body by twisting and pulling until it breaks off. Then, holding the tail in your palm, flex it backwards and squeeze until you hear a crack.

4. Split the tail apart where it cracked and pull a large hunk of meat out of the shell (it looks like a huge prawn). Tear the meat in two pieces to reveal and remove the digestive tract (it looks like a black vein) and the stomach. If the lobster is female, there will be roe at the top ridge of the tail meat (or inside the body cavity). If it is cooked it should be pink; if it is still black, steam the roe for a few minutes before eating.

5. Open the body cavity by sticking your thumbs inside and hinging the legs away from the upper body shell. Here you will find the digestive system which is green when cooked and is called the 'tomalley'. Some people consider this the best bit, but give this a miss if you are squeamish or concerned about digestive toxins.

6. Pull and twist the legs at the joints to remove them from the body as well as the spongy gills. Roll the legs underneath a wine bottle to crush the shells, then pick out meat and suck juices out of the legs.

7. No part of the lobster is harmful, but some parts should be avoided as they taste unpleasant: gills, stomach, intestine, eyes, antennae, antennules and beak.

Arrange flowers

A FLOWER ARRANGEMENT BRINGS A UNIQUE, BEAUTIFUL AND ABOVE ALL, PERSONAL TOUCH TO YOUR HOME. YOU CAN ACHIEVE A CLASSY AND PROFESSIONAL LOOK BY FOLLOWING A FEW SIMPLE RULES.

1. Only use flowers that are fresh, straight and feel firm and vibrant. Discard limp stems or droopy or brown flowers.

2. To prolong the life of the flowers, clean the vase in a dishwasher to ensure it is clean, sterile and free from bacteria. Bottled or rain water is preferable to tap water, as the purification chemicals in tap water can hamper the flowers' uptake.

3. The temperature of the water is important: cool water will make the flowers bloom more slowly and last longer, while warm water will encourage the buds to open.

4. Cut stems under running water at a 45-degree angle using sharp scissors or secateurs. Remove any leaves below the water line as they will rot and pollute the water.

5. If you aren't using oasis, criss-cross a few woody sprigs of greenery at the bottom of the arrangement first to hold the flowers together.

6. Decide on an overall shape for your arrangement, e.g. fan, pyramid or ball. Begin the arrangement by placing structural flowers that will define this overall shape and form the support structure. Don't start adding other flowers until you are happy with your overall structure.

7. Place larger flowers near the base of the group and taller stems near the back, then fill in the gaps with smaller blooms.

8. Use odd numbers of flowers and place the same type of flowers at the same time rather than dotting one kind here and another there, skipping around.

9. Apart from using a cohesive colour scheme you also need to think about shape, sizes and textures and how they interact. Place large and dark flowers at the bottom and lighter, smaller flowers at the top and edges.

10. Make sure each flower has its own space and isn't blocking the view of its neighbours.

11. Don't be afraid to combine buds and blooms with half-open flowers. Buds are very effective at the top of an arrangement.

12. Tall and straight 'line' flowers are useful for creating outline shapes, height and width; 'mass' flowers are usually round and offer colour and variety. The smallest and most delicate 'filler' flowers tie the whole arrangement together with highlights.

PACK A SUITCASE

THE MOST COMMON MISTAKE PEOPLE MAKE WHEN PACKING A SUITCASE IS TO PACK TOO MANY CLOTHES. BEFORE YOU START, PLAN EACH DAY IN ADVANCE AND BEAR IN MIND THAT YOU MAY WANT TO BUY SOME CHEAP CLOTHES AT YOUR DESTINATION. THE MORE CLOTHES YOU PACK, THE LESS ROOM YOU HAVE FOR SOUVENIRS.

1. Gather all the clothes you may need on your trip and spread everything out on a bed or table first, then have a cull – put back at least a third of what you think you need. If in doubt, leave out. Don't pack anything that you don't feel comfortable wearing, otherwise you simply won't wear it.

2. Mix and match so clothes can be worn in combination and if you are uncertain about the weather, pack several layers so then you can dress for both hot and cold weather.

3. Place heavy, bulky items at the bottom, just above the wheels. Then add the non-crease items such as jeans or pyjamas. Leave delicates such as blouses and shirts on top – anything you want to remove immediately and hang up or iron when you reach your destination.

4. Pack shoes in plastic bags to prevent the spread of odours and to stop them dirtying your clothes. Use the space inside your shoes for small items and wrap them in a plastic bag if you are worried about odours. Travel in your heaviest shoes to reduce the weight of your suitcase.

5. Squash underwear and socks down the sides of the case, or if you are a neat freak, roll and fold them and place them in the top netting pockets.

6. Save space by using travel-size toiletries, sealed inside plastic bags in case of leakages.

7. Don't pack valuables in any luggage that will leave your possession during your journey. Keep expensive items with you to ensure they don't get lost or stolen.

8. Rolling clothes can reduce wrinkles (it's the standard way of filling a rucksack). Pack rolled items tightly so they don't unravel and become creased.

9. Place fragile items in the centre, protected by soft clothes.

10. If you are flying, know the weight limit for your airline (usually about 20-25 kg) and weigh your bag at home to avoid paying a hefty fine at the airport.

Mow the lawn

IF YOU LONG TO HAVE A LAWN LIKE CENTRE COURT AT WIMBLEDON OR THE LUSH GREENS OF WENTWORTH, THEN BE SURE THAT YOU ARE NOT CUTTING YOUR GRASS TOO SHORT, DAMAGING THE ROOT SYSTEM AND ENCOURAGING THE GROWTH OF WEEDS. YOU MAY BE DOING THE VERY OPPOSITE OF WHAT IS GOOD FOR YOUR LAWN.

1. Keep the blades of your mower sharp. Lawn care specialists advise sharpening the blades after every four mows, but at the very least you should sharpen or replace twice a year and get the mower serviced regularly. You can tell when it's time to sharpen the blades by looking at your grass: when the tips are torn, white and frayed rather than cleanly cut. Cutting the lawn damages the grass, but it uses more energy to mend a jagged cut than a clean one, wasting resources that could have been used on growth.

2. Remove stones, sticks, dog mess, toys and other obstructions that will damage the mower blade and possibly fly up and hit you in the face.

3. Only mow when the grass is completely dry unless it is so long that leaving it would do more damage. If the grass is damp or long walk more slowly.

4. Edge around the perimeter first and throw the clippings on the lawn, so they can be picked up by the mower. Then start by mowing one or two strips along the entire perimeter; this leaves you room to turn around.

5. Always mow in different directions to prevent graining. Mow in rows or columns; walk all the way to the other side and then turn around. To keep your rows straight, line up a wheel with the line you already made. If your mower has four wheels, overlap each run so that the wheels do not go in the same place and create tramlines.

6. The next time, mow in rows perpendicular to the last mow.

7. Most important of all: don't cut the grass too short. This weakens the root system and leaves grass vulnerable to drought and weeds. It's very tempting when you see weeds like clover, daisies or dandelions growing in your lawn to set the mower on its lowest setting and scalp them, but actually you do more damage to the grass, allowing the weeds to take over. Leaving the grass slightly longer improves the grass coverage and chokes out the weeds.

8. Remove a third of the grass length at a time. If the grass is very long, cut a little bit and then mow again two days later.

9. Mow slopes and shady areas one setting higher than the rest of the lawn.

10. Different varieties of grass have different requirements, including cutting height. For example, bahia grass and buffalo grass prefer 5-8 cm/2-3 in while ryegrass can tolerate 4-5 cm/1 ½-2 in. Stay at the upper end of that range during hot weather or drought and mow closer in cooler weather and before the winter.

11. Allow a petrol mower engine to cool down for ten minutes before refuelling and never fill up on the grass because spilt petrol will kill the lawn.

HOUSETRAIN A DOG

HOUSETRAINING YOUR PUPPY WILL RUN
REASONABLY SMOOTHLY IF YOU ACKNOWLEDGE
RIGHT FROM THE START THAT THERE WILL
BE SOME ACCIDENTS, THAT IT IS YOUR
RESPONSIBILITY TO ESTABLISH A GOOD ROUTINE
(RATHER THAN THE PUPPY'S FAULT FOR GETTING
IT WRONG) AND IF YOU BELIEVE THAT WITHIN
A FEW MONTHS THE PUPPY WILL BE PROPERLY
TRAINED (IT TAKES ABOUT SIX MONTHS FOR A
PUPPY TO GAIN FULL BLADDER CONTROL).

1. Stay calm. You cannot gently and firmly guide your puppy towards the desirable behaviour if you are stressed or a perfectionist. While the puppy is learning you will have to clear up some mess, especially in the morning. If that thought freaks you out, then don't get a puppy.

2. Never punish your puppy for making a mess. It is confusing and may well reinforce the behaviour. There is no point

reprimanding the puppy if you find a puddle or faeces; it's already too late. However, if you see the puppy is about to eliminate indoors, a firm 'No!' and a swift exit will reinforce the appropriate behaviour.

3. Dogs like routine. Establish routines for eating, sleeping and going outside at regular predictable times. Spend as much time as possible with your puppy during the early weeks and take him outdoors regularly.

4. Stay close and watch him, otherwise you will have no idea whether he's been or not and you won't be on hand to praise him. Give lots of praise while he is going and then give a treat afterwards (you can phase the treats out and just verbally praise as he gets older).

5. The more alert and sensitive to his needs you are, the fewer accidents there will be and the more opportunities for success. Look for tell-tale signs: he may circle, go to the door or squat. Pick him up and take him outside immediately.

6. Establish a phrase that you can use when the puppy is outside or on a walk that will encourage him to go – something like 'go wee' or 'go poo'. When he does, repeat the phrase and praise, so he associates the phrase with going to the toilet. You can do the same thing at night before bed – take him outside and say 'go wee'. Eventually, as the dog gets older, he will know that as you prepare for bed, this is his last chance to empty his bladder before the morning, so he will even go to the door ready.

7. As the puppy gets older he will come to you and stare at you, asking for attention. He may need to go out, so ask 'Do you want to go wee?' If the dog responds (gives a little jump, turns to the door, etc.) go and open the door and praise him for asking.

8. Sometimes, ask your puppy 'Do you want to go wee?' in a happy questioning voice as you move to the door. Later you can ask him and he may head towards the door to say 'yes', so you can open the door and give him the option.

9. If you need to leave the puppy alone, leave him in a non-carpeted room such as a kitchen so you can clean up any mess. Just don't leave him for very long. Don't worry, this phase won't last long.

10. Use a special scent-removing pet spray to clean accidents otherwise he will smell the urine and go again in the same place. Some experts advise not allowing your puppy to see you clean up after him, because only subordinate members of the pack would do this.

HOUSETRAIN A CAT

CATS CAN USUALLY BE HOUSETRAINED MORE QUICKLY THAN DOGS. IN FACT, MOST KITTENS CAN GET THE HANG OF USING A LITTER TRAY IN LESS THAN A WEEK, SO LONG AS YOU FOLLOW THESE BASIC GUIDELINES.

1. The ideal length of your litter tray should be one and a half times the length of your cat from nose to the base of its tail, but it is fine to buy an adult litter tray that the kitten can grow into, if you don't want the added expense.

2. Research has shown that cats prefer a depth of about 3 cm/1¼ in of odourless litter in their tray. The tray should be located in a discreet corner (to allow privacy and security) away from food and water, doors, full glass windows, cat flaps and busy areas.

3. As soon as the kitten wakes, gently carry it to its litter tray.

4. Clean the tray every day. You can remove just soiled litter and refresh with clean litter, but every few days you should empty completely and clean the tray with hot water and detergent (beware that some disinfectants are toxic to cats).

5. If you need to relocate the tray, do so gradually, about 20 cm/8 in per day so as not to confuse the kitten.

6. If the kitten messes outside the litter tray, do not scold and punish, which will only teach the kitten to be afraid of you. Also, scolding and then taking the kitten to the litter tray associates the tray with scolding and fear which is the exact opposite of what you want to achieve: privacy and security.

7. Simply clean up the mess thoroughly and use a special scent-removing pet spray so that the kitten is not attracted back to the same spot to relieve itself again.

8. If the kitten continually messes outside the tray then you may have to change something – the kind of litter, or the tray's position or its size; or you may have used detergent with a strong off-putting smell. The most common reason will be that the litter tray is too dirty (it may not appear dirty to you, but your fastidious cat is more discerning than you). Make sure you keep it 'cat clean': change the litter more regularly and see if this helps.

9. If the problem persists, your cat may have a urinary tract infection, so check with your vet to be safe.

Treat stains

EACH STAIN MUST BE TREATED SLIGHTLY DIFFERENTLY, BUT THERE ARE A FEW GENERAL RULES THAT CAN APPLY TO MOST, REGARDLESS OF THE STAIN AND MATERIAL.

1. Start to treat the stain as soon as possible after it happens. The longer a stain remains, the harder it is to remove.

2. Unless otherwise directed, only pre-soak stained fabric in cold water before laundering as many stains can be set by hot water.

3. When applying stain remover, place the stain face down on a paper towel then apply stain remover to the back so that it pushes the stain back out rather than soaking deeper.

4. After pre-treatment, wash the fabric in the hottest water temperature the care label permits and use a biological or enzyme-based detergent.

5. After washing, if the stain is still visible, repeat the stain-removing procedure before the garment dries, otherwise the stain will set.

Oil, fat, gravy or chocolate: Remove as much excess oil as possible with a blunt knife or spoon, apply dishwashing detergent on the back of the stain and leave for 5 minutes to soak into the fabric and break down the grease. Pre-treat with colour-safe bleach before washing in the hottest water allowed.

Lipstick: Blot the stain with a baby wipe or a face cloth moistened with rubbing alcohol.

Milk: Apply a paste of detergent to the back of the stain and leave to soak in cold water for 15 minutes (warm or hot water will darken the stain).

Ink: On cotton, apply rubbing alcohol, then wash; on polyester, spray with hair spray and pat with a clean, dry cloth before washing.

Red wine: Cover with salt then dunk in cold water and blot until the stain disappears, apply colour-safe bleach, then wash.

Tomato (ketchup, spaghetti sauce, etc.): Sponge immediately with cold water, rub with half a lemon, flush with water and blot away the excess. Pre-soak for 15 minutes with a tablespoon of white vinegar, warm water and detergent, then wash at the highest temperature allowed.

Candle wax: Remove as much of the wax as you can with a blunt knife; apply several layers of paper towels or greaseproof paper and press with a warm iron to melt the wax, which should be soaked up by the paper towels.

Chewing gum: Freeze the gum by applying ice packed in a plastic bag or use freezing spray. Chip away as much as you can with a blunt knife then soak in colour-safe bleach before laundering.

Blood: Blot fresh blood repeatedly with cold water or soda water; if it's dried, use a 3 per cent hydrogen peroxide solution.

Fabrics for dry-cleaning: If the fabric is not washable, apply dry-cleaning fluid to the stain with a sponge, allow to air dry, then seek advice from a professional dry cleaner.

A pomander (from French 'pomme d'ambre', apple of amber) is a ball or bag impregnated with perfumes that was traditionally worn or carried to protect against infection and to mask unpleasant odours.

Make a pomander

In medieval times pomanders contained ambergris and had religious significance. Today they are mainly used as fragrant Christmas decorations. The easiest way to make a pomander is with an orange, cinnamon, cloves and a piece of ribbon.

1. Wrap a piece of 15 mm/½ in ribbon around the middle of a large thick-skinned orange, cross it over and bring the ends up as if wrapping a parcel. Fix the ribbon in place using round-headed pearl pins.

2. The orange is now divided into four quadrants. In each quadrant make three separate lines of cloves running from top to bottom, spaced 5 mm/¼ in apart. Just push the clove through the skin until only the head is showing.

3. Sprinkle a tablespoon of ground cinnamon onto the orange making sure it is evenly covered.

4. For extra depth you can add a few optional drops of essential oil. The following complement orange well: bergamot, cedarwood, geranium, ginger, jasmine, lemon, sandalwood and ylang ylang.

5. Place the orange in a paper bag and allow it to cure for a week in a warm dry place.

UNBLOCK A SINK

IF YOU REGULARLY POUR FAT, COFFEE GROUNDS, TEA LEAVES OR VEGETABLE PEELINGS DOWN THE SINK, THE U-BEND TRAP UNDER THE SINK WILL EVENTUALLY BECOME BLOCKED. FORTUNATELY THIS IS ONE JOB EVEN YOU CAN SAFELY DO WITHOUT CALLING A PLUMBER.

1. Remove the plug and fill the basin half full with water. Make sure that the water does not contain cleaning chemicals, as these could splash in your eyes while you are plunging. If necessary, wear goggles to protect your eyes.

2. Use a plunger to release the blockage. Place the plunger over the plughole. Block off the overflow outlet with a damp cloth, so that you can achieve greater suction. Make sure that the inside of the plunger is full of water, rather than air. Water is heavier than air so plunging water is much more effective.

3. With the plunger sealed against the bottom of the sink, plunge up and down firmly several times and then release to allow the water to flow through. Keep plunging if the water level does not fall.

4. When the sink is unblocked, turn on the hot tap and leave it running for several minutes. This will help to wash away any bits that are stuck to the sides of the pipe.

REMOVE THE U-BEND

If the blockage is too large to be cleared with a plunger, remove the U-bend. Clear the area underneath the sink and place a bowl underneath the U-bend.

Unscrew the nut which attaches it to the sink and the nut which attaches it to the waste pipe. Clean the U-bend to remove everything that is stuck inside and reattach and tighten the nuts. Run water through the sink to check for leaks.

If the U-bend is fitted with a clean-out plug, simply remove this to clean the blockage, rather than unscrewing the whole trap.

DRAIN CLEANERS

Make your own drain cleaner by mixing 290 g/10 oz of baking soda with 500 ml/1 pint of white vinegar. Only use a commercial sink unclogger as a last resort. These products contain powerful chemicals that are very harmful to the environment, only provide a temporary fix and corrode metal pipe work. They are also very bad for your health if inhaled.

A plunging action agitates the blockage up and down, and is much more effective than using drain cleaners.

Never pour ammonia and bleach products down the drain at the same time. The chemicals react together to form chlorine gas, which causes acute and irreversible damage to the lungs of anyone who inhales it.

DON'T POUR FAT DOWN THE DRAIN

The main cause of a clogged sink is waste food that builds up in the U-bend. Do not pour hot animal fat down, because as it cools it solidifies and clogs the waste pipe. Even flushing with hot water afterwards may not be sufficient to prevent a build-up of solidified fat.

Carve a turkey

Tidy carving is essential when preparing a turkey dinner to ensure maximum flavour, juiciness and visual appeal.

1. Take the turkey out of the oven and let it rest for twenty minutes before carving, so all the juices go back into the meat.

2. Remove all the strings, skewers and stuffing.

3. Pull the leg away from the body, cut through the skin and keep opening the leg until you can see the hip socket joint.

4. Insert the knife tip into the socket and pull the leg cleanly away from the body.

5. Separate the thighs from the drumsticks: locate the ball joint with your finger and then slice through it.

6. Slice either side of the thigh bone and then remove the bone. Repeat with the other leg.

7. To carve the breast meat, work parallel to the breastbone and cut slices about 5 mm/¼ in thick.

8. To remove the entire breast in one piece, make a cut along the top of the bird's breastbone, then make further slices below this as you gently ease the breast from the body. You can then cut the breast laterally into uniform slices 5-8 mm/¼ in thick.

9. Separate the wing from the body by locating the socket joint with your thumb, then cut through it.

SHOVEL SNOW

SHOVELLING SNOW IS MORE DEMANDING THAN IT LOOKS. IF YOU ARE FIT AND ACTIVE, HALF AN HOUR SPENT SHOVELLING SNOW COUNTS AS A DAILY DOSE OF MODERATE ACTIVITY, BUT IF YOU'RE MORE SEDENTARY, TAKE CARE. HOSPITALS REPORT AN INCREASE IN INJURIES AND EMERGENCY ADMISSIONS FOLLOWING A SNOWFALL FROM OVEREXERTION, INJURED BACKS AND FALLS.

1. Even if you are fit, warm up first with a few stretches so you don't injure yourself in the cold weather. Stretch your back, shoulders and legs (ham strings). Stretch afterwards to warm down.

2. Dress in several layers and wear gloves. Remove one layer at a time to cool down while you work. If you get too hot and

clammy, you will be uncomfortable and this will soon lead to excess heat loss. You want to remain warm and dry (not hot and wet with sweat).

3. Use a good lightweight snow shovel with a long handle (which means less bending) and with a wide non-stick shovel surface. Don't use a garden spade which is too heavy and small and will make you waste energy.

4. As with any repetitive work, your technique is important, as you can easily waste energy if you work inefficiently.

5. Move the snow once. Work out where you are going to put it, so you don't have to move it again later.

6. Use a steady, easy shovelling action at a sustainable pace.

7. Hold the shovel at a slight angle and shovel width-wise along the area. Use your legs as much as possible to lift rather than your back and arms.

8. Keep your back straight as you bend and rise, engage your shoulders and keep one hand close to the shovel blade for better leverage. Be aware of how you move and twist and which areas of your body are starting to hurt so you don't strain your upper or lower back. If your back becomes painful, try to use your legs more.

9. Take frequent breaks and stay hydrated because you can lose a lot of water into the dry cold air. Drink lots of water or better still, a hot chocolate.

10. After clearing, add salt and sand to the area.

REPLACE A BROKEN WINDOWPANE

YOU ARE BOUND TO FACE A TRADITIONAL BROKEN WINDOW AT SOME POINT, SO THIS IS A GOOD WAY TO SAVE MONEY (WITH TIME AND EFFORT).

REMOVE THE BROKEN GLASS

1. First make a star shape on the pane using clear adhesive tape; this will stop the window from shattering when you remove it.

2. Wearing gloves, use a hammer to break the glass and lift away the pieces with your hands. Use pliers to remove pieces of glass from the edges of the pane; you may have to gently waggle slivers of glass to loosen them.

PREPARE THE FRAME

Now the glass has been removed, clean the rebates so that they are free from glass, putty, paint and other debris using a chisel or knife. If the frame is wooden, use pliers to pull out the tiny headless nails (sprigs) which held the old glass in place. For metal frames, the glass was held in place by spring clips – remove these.

BUYING REPLACEMENT GLASS

Make sure you allow for the rebate when measuring up for replacement glass. The glass should be a snug fit, but leave a 2 mm/⅛ in gap around the edges to allow for expansion and contraction of the frame.

PUTTY IN YOUR HANDS

1. Use linseed oil putty for wooden frames and non-linseed oil putty for metal frames. Allow about 140 g/5 oz of putty for every 30 cm/12 in of length.

2. Roll a small ball of putty between your palms until it is malleable. Then roll into sausages and press into the recess. When the panel is fitted, there should be enough putty so that it is forced out of either side of the glass.

REPLACE THE PANE

1. Press the glass edges into the frame and clip in place (metal frame) or nail in sprigs at 20 cm/8 in intervals (wooden frame).

2. Smooth the putty with a putty knife, adding more if required. Make a run-off angle of 45 degrees and use the diagonal edge of the knife to create crisp corner mitres. Cut away excess putty with the knife.

LET IT HARDEN

Allow a week for the putty to harden, two if you want to paint. Paint 2 mm/⅛ in over the putty onto the glass; this will seal the putty against the elements and prolong the life of the window frame.

SEWING ON A BUTTON IS NOT AS PREVALENT A SKILL AS YOU MIGHT IMAGINE. WHETHER IT'S BECAUSE OF BUSY LIVES OR THE LACK OF KNOWLEDGE, DRY CLEANERS AND TAILORS REPORT THAT BUTTON REPLACEMENT IS ONE OF THEIR MOST FREQUENT REQUESTS. TIME SHOULDN'T BE AN ISSUE BECAUSE IT TAKES LESS THAN THREE MINUTES (LONGER THAN IT WOULD TAKE YOU TO DRIVE TO THE DRY CLEANERS).

SEWING A TWO-HOLE BUTTON

1. Use special button thread, which is stronger than ordinary thread. Search online for 'button and craft thread' or ask for it at any fabric store. Match the colour to that used on the rest of the garment.

2. If you can't find the missing button (or it's broken) you

can usually find a spare button on the inside seam of the garment.

3. Use about 30 cm/12 in of thread. After you have threaded it through the needle, double it up and knot the end.

4. Align the holes on the button either vertically or horizontally to match the other buttons.

5. Push the needle through the back of the fabric where the button should be and pull the thread tight until it is stopped by the knot. Thread the needle up through one hole, back through the second and out the back of the fabric again.

6. Check that the button is in the right position, then thread a cocktail stick between button and fabric so you don't attach the button too tightly – you have to leave some room for the buttonhole fabric.

7. Sew through the holes as before, eight to ten times, then remove the cocktail stick and wind the loose thread several times around the shank (the thread between the button and the front of the fabric).

8. Push the needle one last time through to the back, cut the thread, tie a double knot and trim the loose ends.

SEWING A FOUR-HOLE BUTTON

The button is sewed in exactly the same method, except that the stitching forms an x shape (unless the other buttons on the garment have been sewn on using two parallel lines).

Shine shoes

ALWAYS BUY THE BEST QUALITY SHOES THAT YOU CAN AFFORD AND PROLONG THEIR LIFE BY SHINING REGULARLY TO MAINTAIN THE APPEARANCE AND THE QUALITY OF THE LEATHER. YOUR SHOES SHOULD BE CLEANED WHENEVER NECESSARY AND POLISHED AND TREATED MONTHLY. RUB WITH A SOFT CLOTH BETWEEN POLISHING OR USE A SHOE WIPE.

There are scores of shoe-cleaning products, from wipes to sprays, waxes to pastes, but nothing beats good old-fashioned spit and polish.

1. Remove the shoe laces to prevent them getting caked in polish.

2. Remove dried mud and visible dirt with a soft damp cloth and then towel or air dry.

3. Remove white salt stains with a cloth soaked in a solution

of white vinegar – one tablespoon of vinegar in a cup of hot water. Towel or air dry.

4. Cover the entire leather with an even and liberal layer of shoe polish. Apply with a brush or cloth, making sure you work polish well into any cracks and scuffs (stretch the shoe so that you can treat the cracks which commonly run between the instep and toes).

5. Using a separate horsehair shining brush, rub the leather vigorously to remove the excess polish, leaving a shiny film. Remember, you aren't shining the leather; you are shining the polish.

6. Wet a cotton ball and squeeze to remove excess water, then dip in a little polish and rub it on areas of deep shine, such as the toe cap. Spit on the area as you work. This breaks down the polish and helps it to spread more evenly and does the job more effectively than just water.

7. Build up layer upon layer of polish using small circular movements. Take as long and add as many layers as your interest and obsessive need for shiny toes sustain you. Don't use the brush between layers, just keep applying spit and polish.

8. To freshen up the inside of the shoe, sprinkle a little baking soda inside and leave overnight, then remove with a vacuum cleaner.

UNDERSTAND CLOTHES CARE LABELS

INTERNATIONAL CARE LABELS WERE DESIGNED TO BE INSTANTLY RECOGNIZABLE IN ANY LANGUAGE.

What the label should tell you:

- The most appropriate washing method

- The best water temperature

- The safest drying method

- The hottest iron temperature

WHAT THE SYMBOLS MEAN

There are five basic symbols:

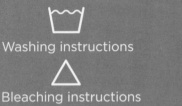

Washing instructions

Bleaching instructions

Dry-cleaning instructions

Drying instructions

Ironing instructions

WASHING

 Machine wash COLD
(no higher than 30°C/85°F)

 Machine wash WARM (no
higher than 40°C/105°F)

 Machine wash HOT
(50°C/125°F)

 One or two bars underneath
the tub indicates that the
garments should be washed
as delicates.

 Hand wash only

 Do not wash

DRYING

 Tumble dry NO HEAT

 Tumble dry LOW HEAT

 Tumble dry MEDIUM HEAT

 Tumble dry HIGH HEAT

 Do not tumble dry

 Line dry

 Drip dry

 Dry flat

BLEACHING

 Suitable for bleaching

 Use a colour-safe,
non-chlorine bleach

 Do not bleach

DRY-CLEANING

 Must be dry-cleaned
A circle with a P inside
indicates to the dry-cleaner
which solvents must not be
used.

 Cannot be dry-cleaned

IRONING

 Iron with LOW HEAT

 Iron with MEDIUM HEAT

 Iron with HIGH HEAT

 Do not iron with steam

Do not iron

DECLUTTER YOUR HOME

CLUTTER IS A MAJOR STRESSOR. IT MAKES BOTH CONCENTRATION AND RELAXATION HARDER, AND MAKES YOU WASTE TIME HUNTING FOR YOUR BELONGINGS – CAR KEYS, TV REMOTE, SCISSORS, MOBILE PHONE CHARGER. WHILE THE PHYSICAL AND EMOTIONAL CLUTTER REMAIN, YOUR LIFE GOES ROUND IN CIRCLES.

1. Do a little decluttering often. If you've got a whole house to sort out, work on one room at a time and don't start something you can't finish (e.g. don't take everything out of a wardrobe and shove it on your bed if you can't sort it in the allotted time).

2. Set a timer and work for between 15 minutes and an hour each day. Spending a few hours a week will make a huge difference to the clutter in your life.

3. Find a place for everything so when you have used it you know where to store it, otherwise you will just throw it in a drawer or shove it to the bottom of a cupboard.

4. Get three large boxes and label them GIVE AWAY/EBAY, THROW AWAY and PUT AWAY. Deal with the first two boxes that day (i.e. list on eBay, take to the tip or charity shop) otherwise you will have stuff sitting in the shed/garage/attic forever.

5. Look to the future rather than defining yourself by your past clutter. By all means keep things which make you proud and acknowledge past achievements, but don't cling onto everything just because it reminds you of your past. Security comes from focusing on the now.

6. Start at the door and work clockwise around the room. This stops you from darting all over the place and getting overwhelmed by the size of the task. It also means that when you take a break you know where to resume.

7. Sort out paper clutter such as post as soon as it arrives. Recycle junk mail immediately, pay bills or schedule payment the same day. Shred bills after one year.

8. If an item has sentimental value, don't confuse this with guilt. For example, if you are only holding onto an unwanted gift because someone gave it to you a few weeks ago, give it away or sell it immediately rather than later.

9. Get rid of anything you haven't used for a year, especially clothes. Throw away old clothes that you plan to slim into, because they only remind you of how you used to be. It is far better to treat yourself to new clothes when you eventually lose weight.

MILK A *cow*

IT TAKES ABOUT HALF AN HOUR TO MILK A COW BY HAND AND IT GETS MILKED TWICE A DAY, MAKING HAND MILKING VERY LABOUR-INTENSIVE, WHICH IS WHY IT'S MECHANIZED THESE DAYS.

However, if you want to try the old fashioned way, you can't sit underneath the cow and just start yanking. First you have to give the cow some food so that it can eat happily while you are milking.

PREPARATION

1. Clean the teats with warm soapy water; this stops contamination of the milk with cow dung, and the warm water encourages the milk to flow. Take a paper towel and wipe each teat dry.

2. When a calf comes up to drink it prods the udder with its nose. This encourages the cow to relax the muscles in its

udder so the milk can flow. This is called 'letting the milk down'. Mimic this action by gently kneading the side of the udder a few times with the heel of your palm.

MILKING

1. Choose two diagonal teats and place a hand around each of them. Clamp the base of the teat between thumb and forefinger. This traps the milk so it can't go back inside the udder and doesn't hurt the cow at all.

2. Now squeeze down one of the teats with a ripple as though you were squeezing a stress ball, starting with your middle finger and ending at the little finger. Do not pull downwards (you may have seen this in cartoons, but it's incorrect and stretches the teat). A little milk should squirt out of the teat.

3. Repeat the squeezing action with your other hand and begin to establish a one-two rhythm.

4. Keep milking for about half an hour – that's how long it takes to empty a full udder.

PERFORM CPR

CPR STANDS FOR 'CARDIOPULMONARY RESUSCITATION' AND COMBINES RESCUE BREATHING AND CHEST COMPRESSIONS TO PEOPLE WHOSE HEART HAS STOPPED PUMPING (IN CARDIAC ARREST).

It delivers oxygen around the body artificially to keep the victim alive until emergency services arrive. These instructions are not a substitute for proper first aid training.

1. Do not perform CPR if the victim is breathing unaided and has a pulse. Put them in the recovery position: lying on their side, supported by one leg and one arm. Lift the chin up slightly to ensure the airway stays open.

2. If the airway is closed and the person is not breathing, begin resuscitation ABC: A=airway, B=breathing, C=circulation.

AIRWAY

1. To open the airway, lift the chin with one hand and push down on the forehead with the other hand to tilt the head back.

2. Look closely for chest movement and place your ear close to the victim's mouth to listen for breathing.

BREATHING

1. If opening the airway does not cause the person to begin to breathe, begin artificial respiration.

2. Tilt the head back, lift the chin and pinch the nostrils together.

3. Breathe in and then seal your mouth over the victim's mouth.

4. Breathe slowly into their mouth.

5. Repeat until help arrives or the victim begins breathing unaided.

CIRCULATION

1. If there is no pulse, call the emergency services before commencing CPR. For children under the age of 8, perform one minute of CPR first.

2. Place the heel of one hand on the middle of the breastbone and the heel of the other hand on top.

3. Lock the fingers and press downwards firmly and quickly about 5 cm/2 in keeping arms straight, then relax and repeat.

4. Perform a little over one compression per second for victims age 8 or over for 30 compressions followed by two breaths of artificial respiration. Then repeat until assistance arrives.

5. For children under 8 years old, do five chest compressions followed by one breath and repeat.

6. It is likely that you will break some of the victim's ribs during compressions; don't panic and don't stop until the emergency services arrive to take over.

MAKE PANCAKES

PANCAKES TASTE GREAT AND THEY ARE QUICK, EASY AND CHEAP TO MAKE. THEY ARE ALSO INCREDIBLY VERSATILE SINCE YOU CAN ADD EITHER SWEET OR SAVOURY TOPPINGS OR FILLINGS.

The perfect pancake mix is simply a smooth batter made out of eggs, flour and milk.

INGREDIENTS

200 g/7 oz plain flour
350-400 ml/12-14 fl oz milk
2 large eggs
1 tbsp vegetable oil
Pinch of salt
Butter or vegetable oil for frying

PREPARATION

1. Sift the flower into a large bowl, make a well in the centre and add the milk and eggs.

2. Gently whisk the liquid until the egg yolks have blended into the milk, then incorporate the flour.

3. Keep whisking until you have a smooth batter, then whisk in a pinch of salt and 1 tbsp of vegetable oil.

4. Coat a crêpe pan, or large frying pan, with butter or vegetable oil and heat the pan on medium heat for one minute.

5. Add a ladleful of batter and swirl it around the pan so that it covers the bottom evenly.

6. Cook the pancake for about 30-40 seconds and then flip it over to cook the other side.

7. Cook for another 30-40 seconds until both sides are golden brown.

8. Transfer to a plate and add your toppings (e.g. lemon juice and sugar/maple syrup/ice cream or cheese and ham).

COOK THE PERFECT STEAK

The traditional approach to steak is to cook on one side until one half is cooked, then flip over once to cook the other side.

However, 3-star Michelin chef Heston Blumenthal has popularized a method which involves flipping the meat every 15-20 seconds so the steak becomes crispy and flavoursome on the outside, without overcooking the centre.

1. Take the steak out of the refrigerator, remove any packaging and allow it to breathe and reach room temperature, then season with a little salt.

2. Place a heavy-bottomed frying pan over a high heat, add a thin layer of olive oil and heat until the oil begins to smoke.

3. Place the steak in the pan and let it fry for 15-20 seconds.

4. Turn the steak with your hands or a pair of tongs every 15-20 seconds (don't use a fork, which will pierce the meat and allow juices to escape). Keep doing this for 2-3 minutes.

5. Remove the steak from the pan and let the meat rest on a wire rack for 5 minutes. This allows the muscle fibres in the meat to relax so that when you cut into the steak the juices won't flood out.

6. Cut the steak into 5 mm/¼ in wide slices with a sharp knife. Season with salt and freshly ground pepper.

Shuck an oyster

WHEN YOU BUY AN OYSTER ITS SHELL SHOULD BE CLAMPED FIRMLY SHUT.

However, when it's time to eat your oyster, the same shell can be very challenging unless you use the correct tools and technique. If you hack away inexpertly you risk breaking the shell into fragments (which you will then have to pick out of the oyster) or spraying water everywhere.

1. Grip the oyster with a tea towel in your left hand (or right if you are left handed) with the round end near your thumb and the pointy end facing your other hand.

2. The pointy end houses the shell's hinge, which you need to break through using a special shucking knife, which is short and wide with a protective guard.

3. Stick the tip of the shucking knife into the hinge and then twist and lever the knife upwards to prise open the hinge.

4. Slide the knife under the long side of the shell to prise it open.

5. Serve the oysters on a bed of ice with some lemon wedges and a dressing of your choice.

MAKE CUSTARD

ONCE YOU KNOW HOW TO MAKE REAL CUSTARD YOU'LL NEVER GO BACK TO THE INSTANT POWDERED OPTION. REAL CUSTARD TASTES CREAMY AND HAS A MUCH RICHER AND MORE SUBTLE FLAVOUR THAN PACKET CUSTARD, AND YOU CAN EVEN USE IT AS A BASE FOR ICE CREAM.

INGREDIENTS

4 free-range eggs

100 g/3½ oz caster sugar

1 tsp cornflour, optional

300 ml/½ pint double cream

300 ml/½ pint full-fat milk

1 vanilla pod

PREPARATION

1. Separate the eggs and place the yolks in a large bowl. (Don't throw away the whites. Use them to make meringues or the Pink Lady cocktail on page 112.)

2. Add the sugar and whisk until the mixture is pale and thick.

3. Add the cornflour and whisk well.

4. Cut the vanilla pod lengthways, peel open and remove the seeds with the back of a knife.

5. Place the vanilla pod into a medium saucepan, add the cream and milk and heat until it nearly boils.

6. Remove the vanilla pod.

7. Slowly pour the hot milk and cream into the bowl and whisk well.

8. Pour the custard into a clean pan and warm over a low heat for about ten minutes, stirring continuously with a wooden spoon until it thickens and begins to steam. The custard is ready to serve when you can draw a clear line through it on the back of the spoon.

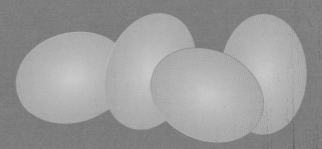

PRUNE SMALL TREES AND SHRUBS

Pruning is one of the most neglected gardening tasks but it is one of the best ways to ensure the good health and sturdy growth of your trees and shrubs, so long as you prune at the correct time of year.

Timing: you can remove dead, injured or conflicting branches all year round, but otherwise prune summer-flowering plants in late winter/early spring while they are dormant; prune spring-flowering plants as soon as their blossoms fade. Check online for specific species of trees.

Flowering shrubs: prune young shrubs lightly by cutting just above a healthy bud. This encourages the lower branches to develop, while the new branch will grow in the direction of the bud. On older, more straggly shrubs, remove branches that touch and compete with each other as well as old and thin branches, to open out the centre of the shrub. If the shrub has been badly neglected you may have to resort to hard pruning by cutting back all the stems to within 4 cm/1½ in of the ground. The following spring, new growth will burst from the base.

Small flowering trees: don't prune newly planted trees (except dead or broken branches) because they need all their foliage to develop their root system. Don't prune the top shoot (the leader). When the tree is a few years old, prune no more than a quarter of the total leaf area in one year. Remove lower branches and any that are too close together.

CLEAN AN OVEN

Unless you have a self-cleaning or textured oven which blasts accumulated dirt and grease into ash, from time to time you'll have to use some serious elbow grease and some nasty chemicals to clean your oven.

COMMERCIAL OVEN CLEANER

1. When using a commercial oven cleaner, always read the instructions and make sure the kitchen is well ventilated.

2. Wear old clothes, eye goggles and rubber gloves. If any of the cleaner gets onto your skin, wash with soap and water for at least ten minutes. If cleaner gets into your eyes, flush with water for 15 minutes before seeking medical attention.

3. Generally, you spray on the cleaner while the oven is cold, wait for a specified period for the chemical to loosen the dirt, then wipe down with a damp cloth.

NATURAL OVEN CLEANER

1. If you value your lungs and hate the idea of using toxic chemicals, mix 150 g/5 oz of baking soda with a few tablespoons of water to make a spreadable paste and rub it into the walls of the oven. Leave to soak overnight.

2. Remove with a wet cloth and scrape away tough residue with a plastic windscreen ice scraper.

3. Finally, spray vinegar onto the surface to remove any last traces of baking soda and have one final wipe down.

VACUUM EFFICIENTLY

EVERYONE THINKS THEY KNOW HOW TO VACUUM A FLOOR, BUT EVEN THE BEST CLEANER CAN ONLY DO ITS BEST JOB WHEN YOU USE IT CORRECTLY.

1. Vacuum at least once a week, or more frequently for high traffic areas or if you have pets that shed, otherwise dust will get kicked around and settle on surfaces, requiring more dusting. Frequent vacuuming also prolongs the life of a carpet by removing abrasive dirt and grit that degrades the pile.

2. Use a crevice tool to reach underneath sofas and into hard to reach places.

3. Dusting and vacuuming throws up dust, so open windows to allow lots of fresh air to circulate.

4. If you vacuum curtains, ceiling fans, light fittings and shelves before you dust them, start at the top of the room and work down. Dust furniture, blinds and windowsills before you vacuum, so the vacuum will pick up fallen particulates or dirt knocked on the floor during dusting.

5. Remove clutter and visible rubbish (like bits of paper, sweet wrappers) otherwise they will block the vacuum cleaner; it's a chore but it prevents damage to the fans and unblocking the vacuum cleaner is a more inconvenient job.

6. Check the bag and filters regularly (extract and bash/wash them to remove dust). Don't let the bag get more than two thirds full or the cleaner will lose suction. If the cleaner makes a strange noise, unplug immediately and check for blockages.

7. Set the correct height for the roller – too low and you'll wear out your carpets. The 'bare floor' setting should not be used on carpets.

8. Vacuum slowly, making several passes before moving on to the next spot. Pass over at least 3 times for light soiling. Use 5-7 passes for heavy soiling and thoroughfares with crisscrossing and overlapping strokes, so that you agitate the pile in several directions.

9. Vacuum rugs from the centre to the perimeter. Don't even attempt small lightweight rugs, which will just get sucked into the machine. Shake/beat them outside instead.

10. On a wooden floor, vacuum in the direction of the planks.

11. Use an edging or brush tool to vacuum the skirting boards, then wipe with a damp rag.

YOU CAN CREATE UNIQUE AND BEAUTIFUL HAND-MADE PAPER BY RECYCLING OLD PAPER FROM LOTS OF DIFFERENT SOURCES: THE CONTENTS OF YOUR PAPER SHREDDER, PAPER TOWELS, PAPER BAGS, NEWSPAPERS OR CONSTRUCTION PAPER – ANY UNWAXED PAPER PRODUCT WILL WORK.

Then all you need is a blender, water, a rectangular frame and a washing-up bowl. The more printed material you use, the more grey your finished paper will be.

1. Make a frame by duct-taping an old piece of metal or plastic mesh onto a small rectangular picture frame. Alternatively, you could bend an old wire coat hanger into a rectangle and stretch a pair of tights over it.

2. Tear five sheets of paper into small pieces and put them into a blender (if the paper is from your shredder bin, just

scoop a few handfuls into the blender). If you are using a lot of printed paper, try to add a few blank sheets (e.g. old envelopes or paper bags) to compensate for the ink.

3. Fill the blender about two-thirds full with hand-hot water and leave to soak for 20 minutes.

4. Pulse the blender several times until the pulp is smooth.

5. Add a teaspoon of liquid starch and a few drops of food dye if you want brightly coloured paper. Blend one more time.

6. After you have finished blending, add in any decorative details such as flower petals, coloured thread, tin foil.

7. Hold the mesh frame over a washing-up bowl of water and then pour the contents into the frame so that the pulp covers it uniformly. You can vary the thickness of the paper depending on how much pulp you use.

8. Shake the frame from side to side below the water so that the pulp levels out and then when you are happy with the coverage, lift the frame out of the water, keeping it horizontal.

9. Place the frame (paper side up) on a towel to soak up the drips and then cover with a hand towel and pat down with a sponge to soak up excess water.

10. Leave the frame in a warm dry place so the water can evaporate.

11. Before the paper is completely dry, carefully remove it from the frame so it doesn't stick, then leave for several more hours until the paper is bone dry and ready for use.

Carve a wooden spoon

THE BEAUTY OF CARVING A SPOON FROM WOOD IS THAT YOU CAN MAKE IT AS FUNCTIONAL OR ROCOCO AS YOU WISH, LIMITED ONLY BY YOUR SKILL AND TIME AVAILABLE.

Sharpen your tools before you start and always keep your hands and fingers behind the path of the cutting tool.

1. Choose your wood. You can carve green, dry or seasoned wood. Green wood is the easiest to carve but it may crack and separate as it dries, destroying your creation. In general, nut trees and hardwoods are better for carving than fruit trees.

2. Select a round log about 10 cm/4 in in diameter and about 30 cm/12 in long and cleave it down the middle using a splitting wedge and lump hammer through the grain and pith, so that you carve with, rather than against, the grain.

3. Remove all the pith and flatten the top surface by tilting the log at a slight angle and making a series of nicks about 4 cm/1½ in apart using a little light wildlife hatchet, with a

short handle. Hold it close to the head for maximum control. Whittle away to two thirds of the way up and then turn the wood over and repeat the process on the other end until you reach a uniform top layer of grain.

4. Create a crank on the bowl end by whittling away the surface so that it slopes down from about a third of the way to the end.

5. Offset the handle end by removing a wide section of timber two thirds of the way on the other (bark) side.

6. Draw a centre line down the top surface and then draw a rough spoon shape with a pencil.

7. Holding the bowl end, whittle down to the handle outline on both sides then carve the shape where the handle meets the bowl. To prevent the wood from splitting at this point, before you carve, make a stop cut from the side vertically down to the pencil line.

8. Next remove material from the sides and front of the spoon bowl by holding the handle and chopping downwards with an axe.

9. Now you have the overall spoon shape, use a series of axe cuts to blend and smooth the back edge of the bowl, then blend the back of the bowl into the handle.

10. Now use a knife for finer whittling to refine the shape.

11. Hollow the bowl with a single-bevelled hook knife, working across the grain.

DRESS @ WOUND

BLEEDING CUTS OR WOUNDS NEED TO BE DRESSED TO PREVENT THEM FROM BECOMING INFECTED UNTIL PROFESSIONAL MEDICAL HELP CAN BE GIVEN. MINOR CUTS AND SCRATCHES CAN BE CLEANED AND THEN COVERED WITH A STICKING PLASTER, BUT YOU SHOULD ALSO SEEK MEDICAL ATTENTION IF A DRESSING IS REQUIRED. FIRST CONTROL THE BLEEDING (SEE PAGE 15).

Call emergency services for abdominal or chest wounds, deep puncture wounds, jagged wounds that won't close, severe bleeding that won't stop after ten minutes of steady pressure or if blood is spurting.

CLEAN THE WOUND

1. Wash your hands and wear sterile disposable gloves if they are available.

2. Run the wound under cold running water and wash around the injury with soap. Rinse the wound until you have removed all visible dirt, grit and gravel. You may have to use tweezers to remove stubborn or deeply embedded particles. Do not dress the wound if there is still visible contamination.

DRESS THE WOUND

1. Apply a little antiseptic ointment.

2. Cover the wound lightly with an adhesive dressing. Fold or cut the dressing so that it just covers the wound. If you are using tape, make the dressing a little bigger so that the adhesive isn't too close to the wound.

3. For shallow, clean lacerations, close the edges of the wound using narrow adhesive strips called butterfly stitches (Steristrips). However, they should not be used in areas of the body where the skin moves a lot (e.g. on joints) or they will tear.

   - Dry the wound before applying the butterfly stitches.

   - Line up the edges of the wound, push them together and apply your first strip in the middle of the wound.

   - Apply an equal number of stitches alternating either side of the first strip, making sure you keep the skin tension uniform and neither too tight nor too loose.

   - After you have applied all the stitches across the wound, add one strip either side of and parallel to the wound to keep them in place.

During the winter few things are more comforting than warming your bones before a roaring fire. However, if your anticipation of a cosy evening is quickly replaced by frustration and failure, you may need to brush up your hearth skills.

1. If the chimney needs cleaning, air will be drawn up the chimney less efficiently and it will be much harder to light, so if you regularly have fires, get it cleaned at least once a year.

2. Remove the fireplace grate and clean out the old ash underneath to give plenty of space to create a draw of air.

3. Replace the grate and loosely scrunch up about twenty sheets of newspaper to the size of tennis balls. Pack them one layer deep on the grate so that they fit snugly together. You may have to wedge in the last few.

4. Throw on a couple of handfuls of kindling and loosely spread them around, followed by a couple of handfuls of coal and two or three small logs positioned vertically and resting against the back wall.

5. If you wish, you can use firelighters or firelighting fluid in addition to your paper and kindling. Follow the instructions carefully – remember these products are designed to be highly flammable.

6. Light the fire and add more logs when the fire is established. Don't add more coal until the fire is roaring.

POLISH WOOD

It is a hard heart that doesn't enjoy the natural beauty of wood, so polishing is the most fun anyone can have with cellulose fibres, lignin and wax and the transformative power of this simple task is deeply satisfying.

1. Wear rubber gloves and open a window so the area is well ventilated (polish contains solvents which evaporate into the air).

2. If the furniture is particularly old and dirty, add a few drops of washing-up liquid to a cup of water and then dip a cleaning cloth into the liquid and gently scrub the dirt away. Dry with a clean cloth to stop the existing polish from softening.

3. Apply antique wax polish to the surface of the wood using a pad of super fine steel wool and a little bit of pressure, scrubbing in little circles, paying special attention to areas where the polish has been worn away. This removes dirt while applying a good even layer of wax. The steel wool won't damage the wood, it will only remove old layers of wax.

4. Let the polish dry for at least half an hour to allow the solvents in the wax to evaporate (see instructions on the polish tin), then buff to a deep shine using dry stockinette cloth which you can buy cheaply from DIY and car care outlets.

TREAT A BURN

FIRST ASSESS WHICH TYPE OF BURN YOU ARE TREATING:

First degree burn: this is the mildest, caused by light scalding or brief contact with hot items (and also includes most sunburn); there will be redness, swelling and pain.

Second degree burn: the skin appears red and blotchy and blisters may form; the burn destroys two layers of skin. Seek medical attention if the burn is on the neck or face, is wider than 8 cm/3 in or has been caused by electricity or chemicals.

Third degree burn: several layers of skin are burned and there may be damage to muscle, fat and bone. The skin appears dry and leathery, coloured white, brown or yellow. Pain is reduced because nerve endings have been destroyed.

TREAT FIRST AND SECOND DEGREE BURNS

1. Place the burned area under cold running water until the pain stops (usually between 15 and 30 minutes). If the victim still feels a burning sensation, it means that the skin is still being damaged.

2. Wash your hands.

3. Apply a cold compress by wrapping ice in a towel, but don't put ice directly onto the skin as this narrows the blood vessels leading to ischaemia (a restriction of blood supply to the tissues) and greater damage.

4. Remove jewellery near the affected area, in case of swelling.

5. Do not touch the burn with your hands or break blisters. Do not use sprays or butter on the burn as this will trap the heat.

6. If the blisters have broken, cover with a sterile petroleum jelly gauze and a bandage to prevent infection.

7. If a limb is burned, raise it as much as possible for the next 48 hours to reduce swelling.

8. The victim may take over-the-counter pain relief such as ibuprofen.

9. Stay vigilant for signs of infection (e.g. fever, pus discharge, increased pain).

TREAT THIRD DEGREE BURNS

1. Call emergency services immediately.

2. Do not remove burned clothing but remove the victim from smouldering materials, smoke or heat.

3. Do not immerse large areas of the body in cold water as the drop in body temperature may send the victim into shock.

4. If the victim isn't breathing, begin CPR (see page 84).

5. Raise the burned area above the heart and cover it with sterile (or clean) cool, moist towels.

Remove A TICK

TICKS CAN CAUSE LOCALIZED INFECTION AND SPREAD SERIOUS DISEASES SUCH AS LYME DISEASE, SO THEY MUST BE REMOVED CORRECTLY WITHOUT SQUEEZING THE TICK'S BODY OR LEAVING MOUTH PARTS INSIDE THE BITE AREA.

1. There are many myths about tick removal. Do NOT use any of the following methods: alcohol, aftershave, cigarette burn, oil, butter, paraffin or petroleum jelly.

2. Only remove with your hands if you cannot locate a pair of fine-tipped tweezers or a tick removal tool.

3. Whichever tool you use do not squeeze or puncture the tick's body, causing fluids to leak into the wound. Try to perform the removal as cleanly and quickly as possible because several failed attempts will stress the tick and cause it to regurgitate potentially infective fluids into the wound.

FINE-TIPPED TWEEZERS

Grip the mouth parts underneath the body and then lift the tweezers vertically away from the skin with steady, even pressure. Do not jerk or twist.

TICK REMOVAL TOOL

This is a little curved two-pronged plastic fork. Slide the cleft of the fork underneath the body between the body and the mouthparts. Twist smoothly 180 degrees as you lift the tool vertically away from the skin with steady, even pressure. Do not jerk.

AFTERCARE

Disinfect the bite site and wash your hands with soap and water.

You could save the tick for future identification, in case you or your pet become infected. Otherwise, dispose of safely.

There are lots of home remedies to treat nausea, so here are some of the most effective ways to settle your stomach.

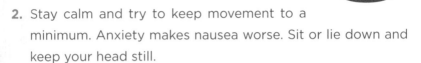

1. Try to figure out the cause of your nausea, which may include food allergies, food poisoning, lactose intolerance, motion sickness, a hangover, pregnancy or an infection.

2. Stay calm and try to keep movement to a minimum. Anxiety makes nausea worse. Sit or lie down and keep your head still.

3. Try lying down on your left side. Bend your knees and remain in the foetal position to ease pressure on your abdomen.

4. Use acupressure. Press your thumb against the inside of your wrist for thirty seconds.

5. Put cool, wet cloths on your forehead.

6. Open windows to let in fresh air and take some deep breaths to help oxygenate your body.

7. For motion sickness, eat dry crackers.

8. Stay hydrated. Drink clear liquids plus peppermint tea, ginger ale or ginger tea; avoid milk, cheese and fatty foods.

9. Dissolve half a teaspoon of baking soda in a glass of water and drink.

10. If nausea persists, seek medical treatment.

Make butter

Making butter at home is a forgotten skill but actually there is very little 'skill' involved. It is extremely simple. You can follow the super low-tech approach, but if you have a food mixer, try the second method.

SIMPLE LOW-TECH METHOD

1. If you still have milk delivered in bottles you can pour the cream off the top into a jam jar (or use shop-bought cream).

2. Seal the lid on the jar tightly.

3. Shake the jar until the cream turns to butter and liquid.

4. Drain the liquid and retrieve your butter. Add a little salt.

FOOD MIXER METHOD

This recipe makes about 0.5 kg/1 lb of butter.

1. Pour 1 litre/2 pints of pasteurised double cream into a cold mixing bowl and whisk on medium speed until it is thick.

2. Keep whisking until the cream collapses into butterfat and buttermilk.

3. Sieve the mixture then transfer the butter into the bowl and whip and sieve again to remove more buttermilk.

4. Add a little salt and then pat the butter with cold wet butter bats to shape into a rectangular block.

5. Wrap your block in foil or greaseproof paper and refrigerate.

USE CORRECT TABLE MANNERS

DINING ETIQUETTE BECOMES MORE ARCANE AND INTRICATE THE HIGHER UP THE SOCIAL LADDER YOU CLIMB AND THE RULES VARY FROM CULTURE TO CULTURE. IF YOU WERE DINING WITH ROYALTY YOU WOULD PROBABLY NEED TO ATTEND A MONTH-LONG COURSE TO REACH THE CORRECT STANDARD, BUT FOR GENERAL GOOD MANNERS YOU SHOULD FOLLOW THESE FOUR BASIC RULES:

1. Be attentive to those around you, especially your host and see what s/he is doing. For example, only start eating when others do. Wait for the host to sit down (or invite you to sit down) before taking your seat.

2. Chew with your mouth closed and do not talk with food in your mouth.

3. Eat slowly and bring the fork or spoon to your mouth rather than your face to the plate.

4. Cutlery: start with the utensil that is farthest from your plate and work towards the centre of your place setting (see page 28).

THE ICING ON THE CAKE

5. Place your napkin in your lap where it should remain for the entire meal and should be used to dab your mouth when required. Do not tuck it into the front of your shirt. If you need to leave the table, leave the napkin on your chair as a signal that you will return. If your napkin drops on the floor, pick it up discreetly. If it is out of reach, ask the server for another one.

6. Keep your elbows off the table while people are eating. You may rest them on the table between courses and while having coffee or tea. You may rest your wrists on the table while eating.

7. Never reach across the table or across your neighbours. If something is out of reach, ask someone to pass it to you.

8. If food is served at the table, pass dishes in a counter-clockwise direction. Use the serving spoons to transfer food from the serving dish onto your plate, not your own cutlery.

9. Never blow on your food to cool it down.

10. Break bread into bite-sized pieces and butter one bite at a time.

11. When you have finished eating, don't push the plate away. Place the knife and fork together across your plate in the 12:6 (UK) or 10:4 (US) position. Partially fold the napkin and place it to the left of your plate.

Make one great cocktail

If you only ever learn how to make one great cocktail, make it the Pink Lady. This gin-based 1930s high society classic is sophisticated, colourful, exotic and velvety; its superb combination of sweet and sour is guaranteed to please.

INGREDIENTS

40 ml/1½ oz gin

10 ml/1 oz apple brandy

20 ml/¾ oz freshly squeezed lemon juice

1 tsp grenadine

1 raw free-range egg white, whipped to a stiff peak

(Many chickens are now vaccinated against salmonella, so while there is never a cast iron guarantee with raw eggs, unless you are extremely risk averse it is a great way for an inexperienced mixologist to add texture, volume and a wonderful creamy frothiness.)

1. Place all the ingredients into a cocktail shaker.

2. Dry shake (i.e. without ice) vigorously for 30 seconds to make the cocktail frothy, then add some ice.

3. Shake again for another 20 seconds.

4. Pour through a sieve into a chilled cocktail glass.

5. Garnish with a Maraschino cherry and serve.

REMOVE A SPLINTER

There are lots of ways to remove a splinter, from baking soda and tweezers to duct tape and white vinegar. One thing you really shouldn't do is squeeze because that may break the splinter into pieces or embed it deeper.

1. First wash the affected area gently with a little soap and water and quickly dry (to avoid the skin becoming soggy). Use a magnifying glass to get a good look at the splinter and its orientation.

2. If an end is sticking out of the skin, grip it with a pair of tweezers and pull in the opposite direction to which the splinter went in.

3. Apply a little Ichthammol ointment (drawing salve) to the area (or alternatively, a pea-sized paste of baking soda and water) and cover with a sticking plaster. The splinter should be drawn into the sticking plaster within 24 hours.

4. For tiny splinters, add a thin layer of white glue to the affected area; peel off when dry, ideally lifting the splinter with the glue.

5. Cover the splinter with duct tape. Leave for a few minutes then peel off.

6. Dip the affected area in white vinegar for half an hour, after which the splinter should rise to the surface.

CLEAN WINDOWS

THE GOOD THING ABOUT CLEANING WINDOWS IS THAT YOU DON'T HAVE TO USE ABRASIVE OR DANGEROUS CHEMICALS. TO FRESHEN UP YOUR INTERIOR WINDOWS A MICROFIBRE CLOTH AND A MIST SPRAY FILLED WITH WATER WILL SUFFICE, BUT IF YOU WANT TO GIVE INTERNAL OR EXTERNAL WINDOWS A REALLY GOOD SPRING CLEAN, FOLLOW THESE INSTRUCTIONS.

1. Place a rolled-up towel beneath internal windows to catch the drips.

2. Fill a bucket with warm water and add a little squirt of washing-up liquid.

3. Wash the windowsill and the window frame before you clean the glass. To remove mildew, use a damp cloth with one part bleach to ten parts water.

4. To wash the glass, dip a sponge or lint-free cloth into the water and starting at the top left of the window clean along and down the window using zigzag movements.

5. Wipe the top and side edges with a dry towel then use a squeegee to remove the excess water with the 'S' method favoured by professional window cleaners.

6. Holding the handle above the rubber blade, start with the blade on the glass on the top left-hand side about 15 cm/6 in from the top so that it points down at a 45-degree angle.

7. Now move the squeegee vertically until the edge of the blade touches the top left corner of the window, then turn your wrist clockwise until the blade is vertical and pull straight across nearly to the top right corner.

8. When the blade is about 15 cm/6 in away from the top right corner, begin to twist your wrist clockwise again so when the right edge of the blade meets the top right-hand corner of the window the blade is at 45 degrees again.

9. Now pull straight down about 30 cm/12 in with the blade tight into the right edge.

10. Return to your starting position by making an 'S' shape, then keep making 'S' shapes as you go back and forth and down until you reach the bottom of the window, leaving a streak-free finish.

11. The squeegee must stay in contact with the glass throughout, so that you perform the movement in one complete stroke.

12. Wipe the bottom of the window frame to remove any remaining water.

CLEAN VENETIAN BLINDS

VENETIAN BLINDS ARE REPUTED TO BE NOTORIOUSLY DIFFICULT TO CLEAN.

Old-fashioned advice involves removing them from the window and soaking them in the bath. Here's a quicker and more methodical way to clean them in situ.

1. Work from top to bottom and left to right. Dust the longer section in between the tilt cords first, followed by the two end pieces.

2. Hold the left end of the slat with your left hand and then with the fingers and thumb of your right hand, clamp a duster against both sides of the slat just to the right of the left tilt cord. Then move your right hand along the slat as you continue to apply pressure, so that you dust both sides of the slat at once. Stop when you reach the right tilt cord.

3. Now dust the two end pieces, working from the tilt cord to an end.

4. If the dirt is ingrained or the blinds are sticky with grease and grime, use a damp microfibre cloth instead of a duster. This won't damage wooden slats so long as the cloth is damp rather than dripping wet. Rinse the cloth regularly in a bowl of warm water so you don't spread dirt on dirt.

CLEAN UPHOLSTERY

Cleaning upholstery regularly is very important because although you often can't see it, the fabric can become suffused with deeply embedded dust. If your sofas and chairs have removable covers, clean them in the washing machine or dry clean. If your covers are non-removable, follow these instructions.

1. Use the upholstery attachment on your vacuum cleaner (usually the one with the brush) and press firmly into the material so that you can suck fine dust through the upholstery as well as on it.

2. You can buy upholstery cleaning products to freshen and remove stains, but you can also use cheap homemade alternatives such as mild laundry detergent and warm water or white vinegar followed by a soapy solution. Baby wipes are also good for removing stains without damaging the upholstery.

3. Clean leather furniture with regular vacuuming (being careful not to scratch the leather with the plastic attachments) followed by a wipe down with a damp cloth. To remove mildew, squirt with a mild solution of white vinegar and water and then wipe dry quickly.

4. If you use commercial leather cleaners, choose wax- rather than oil-based products and spot test them first on a patch of leather that is out of sight.

Preserve flowers

If flowers are a cherished reminder of an important person or event, you don't have to throw them away. So long as you dry them before they begin to droop and turn brown, you can keep your floral memories forever.

1. Choose fresh, healthy flowers and discard any which are wilted or unhealthy as they will look shrivelled and unappealing when dried.

2. Strip the leaves at the bottom of the stem and leave a few closer to the flower bud.

3. Separate each type of flower into individual bundles. Any large flowers should be dried individually.

4. Wrap a piece of string around each bundle, tie with a bow and hang the bundles upside down (flower heads facing the floor) in a cool, dry place.

5. Leave undisturbed for 3-4 weeks until all the moisture has evaporated.

6. To press fresh flowers, arrange the blossoms on a piece of tissue paper and cover with a second piece. Place the tissue flat on a book and then pile several heavy books on top. Leave for three weeks.

7. You can speed up the drying process using a microwave. Lay the blossoms between two paper towels, then microwave on a medium to high setting for one minute.

Get rid of woodworm

Woodworm is the larval stage of certain different types of wood-boring beetle and is often brought into the house in old infested furniture, but the adult beetles can also fly in from outdoors and lay eggs in your home. They are particularly attracted to damp wood and they are often found in damp floorboards and loft rafters. Left untreated over many decades, woodworm can weaken the structural integrity of large areas of timber.

1. The signs of woodworm are lots of tiny holes, typically 1 mm to 1.5 mm in diameter, as well as piles of powdery bore dust (frass) around the holes and surrounding area. Also look for crumbly edges to boards and joists.

2. To check if an infestation is active, paint over the holes with a coat of emulsion during the winter, or cover with masking tape and check in the spring whether any fresh holes have been created by beetles emerging from the wood to breed.

3. Woodworm is usually controlled using chemical pesticides or heating treatment. Normally, both of these methods should be performed by specialist pest controllers but many DIY stores and pest control suppliers sell treatments (although the chemicals are not as concentrated as the ones professionals use). You can treat small infestations by spraying insecticide on the affected areas. The chemicals soak into the wood and kill the woodworm.

Read tea leaves

TASSEOGRAPHY (ALSO KNOWN AS TASSEOMANCY OR TASSOLOGY) IS THE ANCIENT PRACTICE OF INTERPRETING PATTERNS MADE BY TEA LEAVES IN A CUP.

The name comes from the old French and Arabic words for cup, 'tasse' and 'ṭāsa', and the practice can be traced back to Asia, the Middle East and Ancient Greece.

1. Make a cup of tea in a pot (don't use a tea bag or you won't have any tea leaves to read).

2. Pour the tea into a white or light-coloured tea cup and quiet your mind and relax as you drink it. The more you relax and clear your mind the easier your mind will be able to perform pattern recognition and interpret the tea leaves. Take deep, slow breaths in through your nose and out through your mouth.

3. As you continue to drink the tea and ignore distractions, begin to focus on an issue in your life that you wish to explore further or a question that you want to answer.

4. Leave a couple of teaspoons of tea in the bottom of your cup.

5. Holding the cup in your left hand, swirl the tea briskly anticlockwise three times, then quickly tip the liquid onto a saucer.

6. Turn the cup back over and peer into it starting at 12 o'clock and working round clockwise. Be aware of the images and thoughts that pass through your mind (write them down so you can refer to them later). You may also see letters of the alphabet spelled out in the leaves but don't consciously look for them because this process should be predominantly non-linguistic.

7. The first symbol you see represents your dominant character or someone close to you. The next symbol represents the near future. The rim and the middle section represent the things that influence your outcomes. The unifying image that ties the story together can usually be found at the base of the cup.

8. The handle of the cup is called the 'domain'. Images near the handle relate to your home life; those further away from the handle are more strongly associated with 'outside' and 'the other'.

9. Entire books have been written about tea leaf reading, but it is ultimately an exercise in personal creativity and imagination, so you may gain the most benefit from forming your own interpretations and using them to reach a meaningful narrative that addresses your own issues rather than someone else's symbolic repertoire.

PASTEURIZE MILK

Milk is usually safe to drink fresh from the cow, but it can be dangerous for people with damaged, weak or immature immune systems such as children or the elderly.

Pasteurization is the process of heating liquids for a specified time and then cooling quickly to destroy the bacteria that make food spoil. It is named after French microbiologist Louis Pasteur who invented the pasteurization process after realizing that fermentation is caused by the growth of micro-organisms.

1. Pour half a litre of recently boiled water into a large saucepan and then place a slightly smaller pan inside the first pan. This double boiler prevents the milk from scalding and sticking to the pan.

2. Pour your raw milk into the pan and heat on a high hob setting. Use a jam thermometer to monitor the temperature. You need to heat the milk to 63°C/145°F for exactly 30 minutes, stirring occasionally.

3. Remove the milk pan and plunge it into an ice bath. Stir constantly as you cool the milk to 4.5°C/40°F. This will take at least half an hour.

4. Pour the milk into a sterile container (fresh from the dishwasher) and store in the refrigerator.

Make a quill pen

YOU CAN MAKE A QUILL PEN OUT OF ANY LARGE FEATHER THAT FITS COMFORTABLY IN YOUR HAND BUT THE MOST SUITABLE ARE LONG TAIL FEATHERS.

1. Clean the feather with warm water and a little detergent.

2. Scrape a sharp craft knife along the writing end of the feather to remove straggly barbs so you have at least 6 cm/2½ in of clean quill shaft.

3. Remove the paper label from an old soup tin, fill with sand and bake at 180°C/350°F for 30 minutes. Remove from the oven, and stick the quill end into the sand and leave for one hour. This tempering process makes the quill more resilient.

4. To shape the nib, make a cut on the back of the quill that is 1.5 cm/¾ in long at about a 40-degree angle.

5. Make a little nick opposite the first cut to make two horns, then bend the horns together by pressing between finger and thumb until you hear a cracking sound. This creates the central slit that channels the ink.

6. Scrape a sharp craft knife along the sides of the nib to smooth the surface.

Cold smoke cheese

COLD SMOKING IS A GREAT WAY TO ADD FLAVOUR TO ORDINARY EVERYDAY CHEESE SUCH AS VALUE RANGE CHEDDAR.

Hard cheeses are usually more suited to cold smoking (because they melt at a higher temperature than soft cheese) but you can also try smoking mozzarella or Gruyère to add interest to a pizza or soup. The longer you smoke the cheese, the stronger the flavour. Cold smoking makes the fat in the cheese rise to the surface, where it creates a protective layer without melting.

1. All you need to make a home cold smoker is a smoke box and a source of smoke. Buy a large plastic storage container with a lid and an aluminium dryer vent hose from a hardware store.

2. Cut a circular hole in the side of the container the same diameter as the vent hose and push one end of the hose through the hole.

3. Place two or three handfuls of smoking chips on a large sheet of aluminium foil, then wrap it up into a little rectangular parcel and make several holes in the top with a skewer or screwdriver. Place the parcel at one end of a large metal roasting tin.

4. Use alder, cherry, maple, apple or peach wood for a mild flavour; use hickory, oak, walnut or pecan for a stronger flavour. Experiment with different hardwoods, fruitwoods and nutwoods, but avoid pine and softwoods, which contain a lot of sap.

5. Attach the end of the vent hose to the other side of the tin and seal the top of the tin using thick aluminium foil, so that smoke can only escape through the vent.

6. Place 5-10 kg/11-22 lb of ice in the bottom of the plastic container and place the cheese on a wire rack above, but not touching, the ice. Replace the lid.

7. Heat the roasting tin over a low heat. You can use tea light candles or a barbecue set on low.

8. The smoke should fill the plastic box, but the ice will cool it so it doesn't melt the cheese. The melting point of cheese is around 32°C/90°F, so you need to make sure that the wood smoulders rather than bursting into flames.

9. Smoke for between 30 minutes and 2 hours depending on your taste.

MAKE BREAD

MAKING BREAD IS VERY SIMPLE AND SATISFYING AND IS MUCH CHEAPER THAN BUYING AN ARTISAN LOAF FROM YOUR LOCAL FARMERS' MARKET.

INGREDIENTS

500g/1.1 lb strong white flour

2 tsp salt

7 g/1 oz sachet yeast

3 tbsp olive oil

300 ml/½ pint water

PREPARATION

1. Mix the flour, salt and yeast in a large bowl.

2. Make a well in the centre, add the oil and water and mix well.

3. If the dough is too stiff, add another splash or two of water until it softens up.

4. Gather the dough into a large ball and place on a lightly floured surface.

5. Knead the dough for about ten minutes to develop the gluten in it and make it stretchy and elastic. Use the heel of your palm to push and stretch the dough away from you, then pull it back into a ball, turn it 90 degrees and knead again.

6. Gather the dough into a ball and leave in a warm place in a lightly oiled bowl for an hour to rise.

7. Heat oven to 220°C/fan 200°C/gas 7.

8. Place the dough inside a greased medium-sized loaf tin, dust with flour, make a 6 cm/2½ in cut along the top and bake for 25-30 minutes until the crust is golden brown and the loaf sounds hollow when tapped.

9. Tip the loaf out of the tin and leave it to cool on a wire rack.

Make the house ALLERGY FREE

IF YOU OR YOUR FAMILY SUFFER FROM ALLERGIES, ASTHMA OR ECZEMA, THERE ARE LOTS OF WAYS TO REDUCE LEVELS OF DUST, DANDER, PET HAIR AND POLLEN, WHICH ARE SOME OF THE MOST COMMON ALLERGY TRIGGERS.

1. Learn how to vacuum properly (see page 94). The more thoroughly and frequently you vacuum, not only will there be fewer dust mites, but there will also be less dust for the mites to feed on. Make sure your vacuum cleaner has a HEPA filter.

2. Carpets trap dust, so replace them with wooden floors or tiles and use smaller throw rugs that can be cleaned outside the house. This measure alone will reduce the amount of dust beneath your feet by 80 per cent.

3. Use leather and vinyl furniture rather than upholstered sofas and chairs which can also harbour dust.

4. Swap curtains and drapes for blinds, which can be dusted regularly.

5. There are between two and three million mites in the average mattress so cover mattresses with allergen-proof fabric

covers and avoid down pillows. Wash duvets and covers regularly at a temperature greater than 55°C/130°F.

6. Place children's favourite plush toys (which also attract dust mites) in a plastic bag in the freezer for a few hours every other day to kill dust mites.

7. Keep pets out of the bedroom, the place where you spend one third of your life and breathe one third of your air. Vacuum the bedroom more frequently than the rest of the house.

8. Avoid mould by keeping the house dry, washing bathroom walls, shower curtains and cubicles regularly with mould-killing cleaning products.

9. Install an electrostatic air filter to remove airborne allergens.

10. Turn down the central heating and open windows to improve ventilation and decrease humidity.

11. If pollen is one of your allergy triggers, either don't bring fresh flowers into the house or restrict them to flowers with large stamens such as lilies and remove the stamens (which store most of the pollen) outside first.

12. Dust surfaces using an electrostatic microfibre cloth that attracts dust rather than a feather duster which spreads dust into the air.

13. Reduce your exposure to volatile organic compounds (VOCs) such as formaldehyde which are found in a wide range of household items from paint to carpeting. Only buy products labelled 'low VOC' or 'VOC-free'.

Choose houseplants

THE ARE SEVERAL FACTORS TO CONSIDER WHEN CHOOSING A HOUSEPLANT. YOU HAVE TO BALANCE THE REQUIREMENTS OF LIGHT, TEMPERATURE AND HUMIDITY WITH THEIR SAFETY AND LEVEL OF MAINTENANCE. THEIR BEAUTY AND FRAGRANCE ARE ALSO IMPORTANT, BUT THEY ARE MORE SUBJECTIVE FACTORS.

Look at these tables. They show for example that a plant like a Kaffir Lily might be perfect for your lifestyle – low maintenance, average light and temperature requirements – except for that fact that it's highly toxic, so a poor choice if you have pets or children.

There's a wide range of houseplants here. Use the information to start you thinking about the kind of houseplants that would suit your level of expertise, the conditions in your home and your levels of care and enthusiasm.

High light	Medium light	Low light
Aloe Vera	Begonia	Cast-Iron Plant
Coleus	Bird's Nest Fern	Chinese Evergreen
Easter Lily (indirect)	Christmas Cactus	Mother-in-Law's tongue
Polka-Dot Plant	Money Tree	Peace Lily
Agave Plant	Chrysanthemum	Aspidistra
Azalea	Dracaena Corn Plant	Dracaena Janet Craig
Bird of Paradise (indirect)	Kaffir Lily	Dracaena Corn Plant
Cat Palm (indirect)	Arrowhead	Parlour Palm
African Violet (indirect)	Philodendron Imperial Red	

High maintenance	Medium maintenance	Low maintenance
Alocasia	Christmas Cactus	Aspidistra
Baby's Tears	African Violet	Dracaena Janet Craig
Hibiscus	Arrowhead	Dracaena Corn Plant
Jasmine	Easter Lily	Parlour Palm
Cat Palm	Money Tree	Chrysanthemum
	Philodendron Imperial Red	Kaffir Lily
	Rubber Plant	

High humidity	Medium humidity	Low humidity
Alocasia	Aspidistra	Agave Plant
Christmas Cactus	Dracaena Corn Plant	Aloe Vera
Chrysanthemum	Parlour Palm	Asparagus Fern
Dracaena Corn Plant	Bird of Paradise Plant	
Azalea	Cat Palm	
Arrowhead	African Violet	
Money Tree	Bleeding Heart Vine	
Coffee Plant	Rubber Plant	
	Umbrella Plant	

Highly toxic	Toxic but not deadly	Very low toxicity
Alocasia	Chrysanthemum	Jasmine
Agave Plant	Aloe Vera	Dracaena Corn Plant
Azalea	Bird of Paradise Plant	Aspidistra
Kaffir Lily	Coffee Plant	Dracaena Janet Craig
Arrowhead	Rubber Plant	Christmas Cactus
Easter Lily	Umbrella Plant	Parlour Palm
Philodendron Imperial Red	Asparagus Fern	Cat Palm
Bleeding Heart Vine		African Violet
		Money Tree

CREATE HOMEMADE CANDLES

CREATING CANDLES AT HOME IS SIMPLE AND THERE'S LOTS OF SCOPE TO ADD SCENTS AND COLOURS TO MAKE THEM UNIQUE.

1. There are three main types of wax for your candles: paraffin wax (which is the cheapest and most common and can easily be scented and coloured); soy wax, which is made from soy beans, is eco friendly and burns more slowly, and beeswax which has air purifying qualities but doesn't take colour or scent very readily.

2. You can also use the leftovers of old candles rather than throwing them away.

3. Cut the wax up into pieces so it will melt more easily.

4. Create a double boiler by putting boiling water in a large pan and then placing a smaller pan inside. Tip the fragments of wax into the smaller pan and place the large pan on the heat so that the water boils.

5. Use a sugar or meat thermometer to make sure the wax doesn't overheat and ignite.

   • Paraffin wax should be melted between 50 and 60°C/122 and 140°F.

   • Soy wax should be melted between 77 and 82°C/170 and 180°F

   • Beeswax should be melted between 63 and 77°C/145 and 170°F

6. When the wax is liquid and clear add a few drops of essential oil, for scent, and oil-based dyes. Don't use water-based dyes such as food colouring.

7. Tape the wick to the bottom of your candle mould.

8. Trap the top of the wick between two pencils, tape them together and place them on top of the mould so they keep the wick vertical.

9. Pour in your molten wax and leave to cool for 24 hours.

10. Carefully separate the pencils and trim the exposed wick to 5 mm/¼ in.

MAKE JAM

JAM-MAKING BEGAN A FEW CENTURIES AGO AS A WAY OF PRESERVING FRUIT THAT WOULD OTHERWISE ROT AND GO TO WASTE.

Back then jam was a luxury item because sugar was a very expensive 'spice' that had to travel half way around the world before it could be enjoyed by very wealthy Europeans. In the New World maple syrup, honey and molasses were used instead of cane sugar.

Here's a very simple recipe that uses just two ingredients: sugar and raspberries. Raspberries are high in pectin, so you don't need to add any extra to make your jam set. The best jam is made rapidly in small quantities and as long as you sterilise your jars properly your delicious product should taste fresh for up to six months.

INGREDIENTS

450 g/1 lb raspberries, fresh (or slightly under ripe)
and good quality (don't use bruised or second-rate fruit)
450 g/1 lb granulated sugar

PREPARATION

1. Sterilise three 300 ml jam jars and lids by running them through the dishwasher on the hottest cycle. Alternatively, wash with warm soapy water, rinse well and then bake in the oven at 140°C/275°F/gas 1 for at least 20 minutes.

2. Place some saucers in the freezer for half an hour to chill; you will need them later to test whether the jam has reached setting point.

3. Place the sugar and raspberries into a low-sided, wide stainless-steel saucepan (so the jam cooks quickly) over a very low heat. Don't use an aluminium pan, which will affect the taste.

4. Keep stirring until all the sugar has dissolved. Don't allow the sugar to burn. You just want to melt, not caramelize or burn it. For even quicker results, you could heat the sugar in a moderate oven for fifteen minutes before adding to the pan.

5. Now bring the mixture to a rapid rolling boil and cook for 3-5 minutes until the jam starts to thicken and bubble more slowly as it approaches its setting point.

6. Remove the pan from the heat to test. Put a little jam on a chilled saucer from the freezer and leave to cool for a few minutes. Then stick your finger into the jam. If the jam wrinkles it is ready. If not, place it back on the heat.

7. Transfer the jam to your sterile jars. Do not add hot jam to cold jars otherwise the glass may shatter. Put the lids on while the jam is still hot.

MAKE SOAP

SOAP IS MADE BY MIXING A STRONG ALKALI (USUALLY SODIUM HYDROXIDE FOR HARD SOAP), WHICH IS HIGHLY SOLUBLE IN WATER, WITH A FAT OR OIL AND THEN HEATING.

The fat or oil contains fatty acids which react with the alkali to form glycerol. Then the sodium joins with the fatty acids to form a compound called sodium stearate, which is soap. The glycerol helps set the soap and is also a good skin moisturizer.

1. Wear old clothes, rubber gloves and goggles and be very careful of splashes and spillages. You will be using dangerous caustic materials. Make the soap in a well-ventilated room.

2. The common names for sodium hydroxide are lye and caustic soda, which you should be able to buy from a hardware store. Make sure you buy 100 per cent sodium hydroxide and not a cleaning product that also contains other chemicals.

3. Pour 500 ml/17 fl oz tap water into a clean bucket. Slowly add 165 g/5½ oz of caustic soda to the water while stirring.

As the caustic soda reacts with the water, the liquid will heat up. Do not breathe in the fumes.

4. Now heat 340 g/12 oz of coconut oil (or beef tallow – see page 144) in a large saucepan over a low heat. When it has melted add 440 ml/15 fl oz each of sunflower oil and olive oil and heat the liquid to about 50°C/20°F (use a glass thermometer).

5. Keep stirring until all the oil has blended, then pour it into the bucket and stir for about 40 minutes until the soap mixture thickens ('traces') and turns opaque. You can tell when the soap is tracing when you draw a line across the surface and a trace remains for a few seconds.

6. Now is the time to stir in any extra perfumes, essential oils or decorative elements such as flowers, honey, orange zest, cinnamon, etc.

7. Pour the mixture into moulds, which can either be smaller individual shapes or one large rectangular container (you can cut the soap into smaller blocks when it has set). Leave the soap to cool for 24 hours.

8. Remove the soap from the moulds and leave to dry in a cupboard for a month so any remaining caustic soda dissolves and the soap becomes milder.

Weave a basket

BASKET WEAVING IS ONE OF THE MOST ANCIENT HUMAN CRAFTS AND THE OLDEST BASKETS HAVE BEEN CARBON DATED TO BETWEEN TEN AND TWELVE THOUSAND YEARS AGO. BASKETRY AND POTTERY HAVE BEEN CENTRAL TO THE DEVELOPMENT OF HUMAN CIVILIZATIONS.

Some archaeologists argue that weaving may have formed one of the earliest human models of mathematics and engineering, because of its reliance on number, pattern and structure.

Here's a simple method to create a rectangular basket from flat reeds of sugar maple wood.

1. Soak the reeds for about ten minutes. Lay five horizontal reeds in place on the table, spaced equally apart. Use a spoke weight (an extra thick heavy ruler) to weight them down and to measure the spacing.

2. Now thread seven reeds perpendicular to the first five using

an under-over weave: the first reed goes over the first, under the second, over the third, under the fourth and over the fifth. The second reed goes under the first, over the second, under the third, over the fourth and under the fifth. The third reed is woven like the first and so on.

3. If woven correctly, the square should hold together under its own tension. This will be the base of the basket.

4. Twine a 'keeper row' on your basket base. Take a piece of round reed about 1 m/3 ft 3 in long and crimp it in the middle with a pair of pinch nose pliers. Then bend at this point and place the loop over one of the middle reeds so you have a double reed. Weave the top and bottom reeds alternately around the rectangular base to secure the structure.

5. Soak the base and sides in water for ten minutes to make them pliable, then bend the reeds upwards to put a good crease where the base becomes the sides.

6. Now weave horizontal reeds of pre-soaked maple to build up the sides.

7. You can weave the side reeds butted up against each other, or you can leave gaps between them, depending on the style.

8. At the top of the basket weave a rim row and then bend the top ends of the reeds over at the rim and tuck the ends down underneath the second row from the top. If they are too long, cut them first so that they fit into place without any excess.

Tease, card & spin wool

ONCE A FLEECE HAS BEEN WASHED IT MUST BE TEASED TO REMOVE ANY REMAINING BITS OF DIRT OR IMPURITIES (SUCH AS TWIGS, GRASS, ETC.) AND CARDED TO LINE UP ALL THE FIBRES BEFORE IT IS FINALLY SPUN INTO YARN.

TEASING

Open up a large lock of wool by pinching it and making quick side to side pulling movements to fluff up the wool to allow ingrained dirt to fall to the floor. You may also have to pick out larger objects by hand.

CARDING

Carding cleans the wool further and lines up the fibres. Carding by hand requires two wooden rectangular paddles with fine metal bristles. Brush a handful of wool from your hand onto one of the paddles and then scrape the other paddle across it several times in the same direction. When the wool is straight and evenly distributed on both paddles, scrape in the reverse direction so that all the wool ends up back on the first paddle. The resulting 'rolag' of wool is ready for spinning.

SPINNING

The wool fibres have tiny scales on them which interlock with each other when you twist them around. Spinning them makes the fibres hook together to give them collective strength.

The simplest way to spin wool is using a drop spindle, which is a lightweight wooden disc with a piece of dowel stuck through the middle (a spinning wheel uses the same principle, except the wheel is operated by a foot pedal).

1. Take a 50 cm/20 in piece of yarn and tie an overhand knot in it so that the yarn forms a loop. This will be your 'leader yarn' that is used to start the twist.

2. Attach the leader yarn to the spindle using a slip knot and then feed the end of the rolag through the other end.

3. Introduce twist into the yarn by rolling it from the top of your thigh to your knee.

4. Let go of the spindle and allow the spin to spread up the yarn so that the end of the rolag is 'drafted' to become about 20 cm/8 in of twisted yarn.

5. Keep a little triangle at the end of the rolag and pinch it so the spin doesn't transfer too far.

6. When you have about 60 cm/24 in of yarn, wrap it around the spindle (beneath the disc) and then repeat the process to create the next section of yarn.

Read palms

PALMISTRY, OR CHIROMANCY, IS THE ANALYSIS OF PEOPLE'S CHARACTER AND LIFE EXPERIENCES, OR FORETELLING THE FUTURE, BY INTERPRETING THE FEATURES AND LINES ON THEIR PALMS.

It has been practised in many Eastern cultures for several thousand years. The Hindu sage Valmiki, author of the famous epic Rāmāyaṇa, is believed to have written a work on palmistry during the first millennium BC. There are many different traditions and interpretations, but the three major lines on everyone's palm are the Head Line, the Heart Line and the Life Line.

Head Line: starts at the edge of the palm just below the index finger and runs across the palm. It represents the mental state and how a person thinks (rather than intelligence), beliefs, philosophy and approach to life.

- Deep long line across the palm: logical thinker, realist; thinks a lot before making a decision

- Short line: simple, decisive thinker; quick and to the point

- Curved line: creative and flexible thinker; generator of ideas